Cameroon

WORLD BIBLIOGRAPHICAL SERIES

General Editors:
Robert L. Collison (Editor-in-chief)
Sheila R. Herstein
Louis J. Reith
Hans H. Wellisch

VOLUMES IN THE SERIES

VOLUME 63

Cameroon

Mark W. DeLancey
Peter J. Schraeder
Compilers

CLIO PRESS

OXFORD, ENGLAND · SANTA BARBARA, CALIFORNIA
DENVER, COLORADO

British Library Cataloguing in Publication Data

DeLancey, Mark W.
Cameroon: a bibliography. – (World bibliographical series; V.63)
1. Cameroon – Bibliography
I. Title II. Schraeder, Peter III. Series
016.967'1104   Z3761

ISBN 1–85109–006–1

Clio Press Ltd.,
55 St. Thomas' Street,
Oxford OX1 1JG, England

ABC-Clio Information Services,
Riviera Campus, 2040 Alameda Padre Serra,
Santa Barbara, Ca. 93103, USA

Designed by Bernard Crossland
Typeset by Columns Design and Production Services, Reading, England
Printed and bound in Great Britain by
Billing and Sons Ltd., Worcester

THE WORLD BIBLIOGRAPHICAL SERIES

This series will eventually cover every country in the world, each in a separate volume comprising annotated entries on works dealing with its history, geography, economy and politics; and with its people, their culture, customs, religion and social organization. Attention will also be paid to current living conditions – housing, education, newspapers, clothing, etc. – that are all too often ignored in standard bibliographies; and to those particular aspects relevant to individual countries. Each volume seeks to achieve, by use of careful selectivity and critical assessment of the literature, an expression of the country and an appreciation of its nature and national aspirations, to guide the reader towards an understanding of its importance. The keynote of the series is to provide, in a uniform format, an interpretation of each country that will express its culture, its place in the world, and the qualities and background that make it unique.

SERIES EDITORS

Robert L. Collison (Editor-in-chief) is Professor Emeritus, Library and Information Studies, University of California, Los Angeles, and is currently the President of the Society of Indexers. Following the war, he served as Reference Librarian for the City of Westminster and later became Librarian to the BBC. During his fifty years as a professional librarian in England and the USA, he has written more than twenty works on bibliography, librarianship, indexing and related subjects.

Sheila R. Herstein is Reference Librarian and Library Instruction Coordinator at the City College of the City University of New York. She has extensive bibliographic experience and has described her innovations in the field of bibliographic instruction in 'Team teaching and bibliographic instruction', *The Bookmark*, Autumn 1979. In addition, Doctor Herstein co-authored a basic annotated bibliography in history for Funk & Wagnalls *New encyclopedia*, and for several years reviewed books for *Library Journal*.

Louis J. Reith is librarian with the Franciscan Institute, St. Bonaventure University, New York. He received his PhD from Stanford University, California, and later studied at Eberhard-Karls-Universität, Tübingen. In addition to his activities as a librarian, Dr. Reith is a specialist on 16th century German history and the Reformation and has published many articles and papers in both German and English. He was also editor of the *American Society for Reformation Research Newsletter*.

Hans H. Wellisch is a Professor at the College of Library and Information Services, University of Maryland, and a member of the American Society of Indexers and the International Federation for Documentation. He is the author of numerous articles and several books on indexing and abstracting, and has also published *Indexing and abstracting: an international bibliography*. He also contributes frequently to *Journal of the American Society for Information Science, Library Quarterly*, and *The Indexer*.

For Blaine, Mark and Elise
and
For William and Helen Schraeder

Contents

ix

Contents

Introduction

In two important respects the recent history of Cameroon has been different from many of the rest of the countries of Africa. Cameroon's economy has been characterized by long term growth and some development, aided by the discovery of petroleum and capable economic planning. Even during the ongoing drought, Cameroon has been largely food self-sufficient. Moreover, with the exception of one serious attempted *coup d'etat*, the political situation has been marked by stability, though the political system cannot be described as democratic. There is, however, movement toward and some promise of democracy under the current leadership of the country's second president, Paul Biya.

However, in many respects, Cameroon is typical of other African states. Although its 1980 population of 8.1 million puts it in the upper third of African countries, Cameroon is located closer to the median with respect to most measures. A survey of 47 African states in 1980 reported 19 countries with per capita incomes higher, and 27 lower, than Cameroon's $328. Twenty-six countries had a higher average population density and 20 a lower density than Cameroon's 16.2 persons per square kilometre.

These averages may be misleading, for there are substantial variations in density and income between the provinces of Cameroon. Too, there are great variations within provinces, both between rural and urban and between different rural areas. The highest density zones are located in areas of derived savanna, light forest, and urban centres. The lowest densities are found in forested regions.

There are also very great variations in income. One study reports that 10 percent of the population receive 60 percent of the national income – or 90 percent of the population receive only 40 percent of the income. Lowest incomes are in the North, East, and North-West; highest incomes are in the most urbanized provinces. See USAID *Country development strategy statement FY 82*, (Washington IDCA, 1980) and 'The political economy of regional development in Cameroon' in *An African experiment in nation-building* (q.v.). Urban dwellers receive a large amount of the national income, and rural dwellers receive only a very small proportion.

Twenty-eight percent of the population live in urban areas, although 80 percent of the economically active population are involved in agricultural activities. The significant differences between urban and rural life are indicated by measures of electricity use – 23 percent of urban and 1/2 percent of rural dwellers; pipe-borne water, 58 percent of urban and 8 percent of rural dwellers; and, corrugated metal roofs, 83 percent of urban and 36 percent of rural inhabitants. The concentration of amenities in the urban areas is continuing to increase. See *Main results of the April 1976 general population and housing census* (q.v.).

The population of Cameroon consists of numerous ethnic groups; some estimates suggest that there are as many as 200 identifiable ethnic entities. Unlike the Nigerian situation, no one of these groups represents a politically significant proportion of the population. However, two other aspects of diversity within the population are of political importance – the division between English-speaking and French-speaking Cameroonians which results from the colonial history of the state and the potentially more significant division between North and South which is the result of pre-colonial, colonial and post-independence factors. The anglophone-francophone conflict serves largely to weaken the Southern side in the Northern-Southern division, for the large majority of the anglophone population lives in the South. Such conflicts are real, however, only when exploited by élites or potential élites. In a sense, these are resources that might be mobilized by political leaders.

As in most West African countries, Cameroon stretches from the humid Atlantic coast with its very high rainfall to the interior of the continent with its dry desert climate. Altitude variations combine with these climate variations to yield five main regions of agricultural production, each characterized by certain major crops. The plateaus and savannas of the North produce millet, groundnuts, rice and cotton. Maize, cassava, yam, sweet potato and market garden crops are of some importance. Cattle, sheep, goats and horses are raised in large numbers. Fishing on Lake Chad, the Logone River and the Benue River provides some protein. There is no forest production. The western plateau produces maize, tubers, plantains, groundnuts and market garden items. It is also an important region for the production of Arabica and Robusta coffee. Cattle are raised and there has been an interesting and successful development of pisciculture in recent years. There is little forest production. Tea, rice and chinchona are in various stages of development.

The central savanna region produces large amounts of food crops (maize, yams, cassava, plantains and sweet potatoes) and cash crops (cocoa, coffee, tobacco and sugar). Small but important productions of gourd seeds and sesame seeds also occur here. Rice is being developed and cotton experiments are being conducted. Cattle are raised in the North Eastern part of the region and there are good timber stands, particularly at Deng-Deng.

The rain forest region of the South produces large amounts of food – plantain, cassava, cocoyam, groundnuts – and it is the major producer of cocoa. Oil palm products are grown and there is a suitable environment for the extension of Robusta coffee plantings. Cattle cannot be raised here, but small livestock production takes place and may be expanded. Fishing and hunting provide limited amounts of protein. The nation's forestry industry is centered in this area.

Food production in the coastal region is similar to that of the southern forest area, but large-scale development of agro-industrial plantations is a major feature. Oil palm, rubber, bananas, tea and pepper are currently produced on these estates, and experiments with coconut, pineapple and avocado are being conducted. Some coffee is grown on the sides of Mt. Cameroon. Sea and river fishing are important and the significant timber industry continues, although resources are now becoming depleted. There is a small amount of animal husbandry.

Cameroon has a rather low proportion of its land under cultivation. Overall, it is estimated that 3.2% of the total surface area of the country is presently being cultivated. One study indicated that 6% of the country was being utilized for agriculture, 17% for grazing, 18% was fallow and 50% was forest. The remaining 9% were water surface and waste lands. See Mary T. Chambliss' 'Cameroon's agricultural economy in brief'. In any case, it appears that the Republic of Cameroon might greatly increase production by extending the areas presently under cultivation.

Aside from other problems, some people argue that a major

difficulty in fulfilling such a proposal is Cameroon's small population. However Cameroon's population policy aims at an increase from the present figure of 9 million to about 18 million persons. One is impressed by the conviction widely held among members of the Cameroon élite that such population growth is necessary 'to provide the labor needed for our economic growth'. Government perceptions of the country's population size and rate of growth are that it is low. In the past Cameroon continued French colonial policies outlawing contraception and added new legislation in this respect. There are more recent indications that official attitudes in this respect are changing.

With its wide variety of agricultural environments, its large amount of land still not under cultivation, and the relatively low level of technology of most of its farm population, Cameroon would appear to have an important potential as an agricultural producer. This potential could be utilized to serve the needs of Cameroon's neighbours, most of which are already food-deficit states with rapidly increasing needs for food products. At this time, Cameroon produces sufficient food for its needs, and some food is exported (often illegally) to neighbouring states. With appropriate development planning and action, Cameroon could greatly increase food production, increase rural incomes and provide an important financial contribution to self-development.

A major impediment to the development of the country is the present condition of the transportation network. The extension of the Trans-Cameroon railway to Ngaoundere opened up large areas which were previously ill-served and the minor extension to Kumba connected an important food-producing area to the urban site of Douala. The road system, although expanded in recent years, is still inadequate in most regions. Particularly in the coastal areas, where rainfall ranges from 200 to 400 cm or more per year, the maintenance of unpaved roads is very difficult, and many roads remain out of service for long periods. In the cities roads are generally paved and well-maintained, but in rural areas there are many regions not even served by the most rudimentary of farm-to-market roads. In many cases local villages have attempted to increase food production for sale to urban or foreign markets, but have found it impossible to market the produce due to transportation difficulties. Road connections to Nigeria and Gabon are extremely weak.

In addition to agriculture and forest production, Cameroon has iron, bauxite and petroleum resources. Only petroleum is now being exploited, mostly for export. Current domestic needs are processed at a local refinery which opened in 1980. Liquid natural gas may be exported. Cameroon will thus have an important income earning ability through the export of crude and refined products for some years to come. At present the refinery and most known exploitable reserves are located in the anglophone portion of the country.

There is a moderate range of industrial production in the country, the most important element of which is aluminium (based on imported bauxite). Other products include fertilizer, pulp and paper, plywood, plastics, beer, cigarettes, chocolate and a variety of other items. It is estimated that 20 percent of GDP is derived from industry, 33 percent from agriculture and 47 percent from services.

The country is dependent upon imports for machinery and other manufactured goods. Major exports include petroleum, cocoa, coffee, timber and aluminium; coffee and cocoa represent 65 percent of the value of exports. The EEC receives 60 percent of Cameroon's exports and is the source of 68 percent of imports. France, the ex-colonial power for most of the country, receives 22 percent of exports and provides 45 percent of the imports. The trade balance has registered small deficits in some years but growing petroleum production has led to regular, if small, surpluses.

Cameroon has an agricultural potential and is situated near food-deficit states, there is no excess population problem although there is an absence of technology and skills, and there are some valuable mineral resources, including petroleum. There are numerous obstacles, but Cameroon can be a viable economic entity with the possibility of economic growth and development.

German Cameroon

Cameroon has experienced diverse external influences in its recent history. In the 15th century Portuguese explorers sailed along the coast and opened trade relations. Other traders – Spanish, French, British, American and German – became active first in the slave trade and later in the legitimate commerce in ivory, rubber and other primary products. Major influences were also exerted by African incursions, such as the movement of the Fulani into the north in the 18th century and their conquest of that region in the early 19th century, see *Fulani hegemony in Yola* (q.v.). It was, however, the Germans who in 1884 established themselves as the colonial power in Cameroon. During the next thirty years, the German protectorate greatly extended in size, far beyond the present-day borders of independent Cameroon.

The German period of rule was significant in many ways. For example, much of the basic infrastructure of the country was established during this time. Moreover, the process of drawing the territory into the international capitalist economic system and the establishment of economic dependence upon Western Europe was furthered. Also, it was during this time that an attitude of administrative dominance and paternalism over the rural populations was established, an attitude that has continued through German, British and French periods of rule, and is still in evidence in independent Cameroon. This is probably less true of the British than the French, German or Cameroonian administrations. Through their wanton neglect of the territory, the British gave the rural dwellers more chance for initiative.

In the German period the two major economic activities of the protectorate were trade and plantation agriculture. European proponents of each system of exploiting local resources conflicted constantly over scarce labour and in their attempts to pass legislation favourable to their view. Trade, mainly in rubber, ivory and palm products, was conducted between European agents and Cameroonians who gathered the produce from wild sources. Very little cultivation was involved, although there were some limited attempts to train Africans in proper rubber tapping methods and agricultural techniques. Large numbers of labourers were involved in gathering this produce and in head-carrying it to shipping points. This caused substantial dislocation in the hinterland and greatly disrupted agricultural processes in the affected areas.

In South Western Cameroon the extensive development of plantations was the cause of large-scale and widespread migration. The plantations were the cause of great suffering, misery, and death during the German rule of Cameroon. Plantations need extensive areas of land and large, inexpensive supplies of labour. The first requirement leads to development in areas of low population density, with the local population usually displaced (in Cameroon to reservations). The second requirement involves migration from areas of high density. This migration, which to a large extent was forced, was the cause of much human hardship. German explorers found potential workers in inland areas which differed in vegetation, climate and disease vectors from the coastal regions where the plantations were located. One might characterize the supply areas as healthy, but the plantation areas were definitely unhealthy.

During the First World War the allied powers invaded the territory, drove the Germans out, and divided the land between them. In 1922 the two areas became League of Nations mandates and in 1946 United Nations trust territories. French Cameroon became an independent state in 1960, and the southern portion of British Cameroons joined it on October 1, 1961 to form the Federal Republic of Cameroon. The northern portion of British Cameroons became a part of Nigeria. On June 2, 1972 the federation was ended and a unitary state, the United Republic of Cameroon was formed. President Biya altered the name to the Republic of Cameroon (RC) in 1984.

Anglophone Cameroon

After the removal of the Germans, the British took control of the South Western and North Western portions of Cameroon. That portion which later became part of the RC was generally neglected by the British. It was a small territory with little or no apparent value in British eyes, and because of its mandate/trustee-ship status its position in the British Empire was never considered secure or permanent. There was neither desire nor interest on the part of the British, and, as a result, little effort or funds were invested in the territory. For most of the period, Southern Cameroons, as the area was entitled, was treated as a colony of Nigeria, which was a colony of Britain. The movement into Cameroons of Nigerians, especially Ibos, Ibibios and Efiks, became very pronounced and this was to be a major factor in the decision of the inhabitants of Southern Cameroons to join Cameroon rather than Nigeria in 1961. The fear of Nigerian, especially Ibo, domination and exploitation was very great. The Ibos became a predominant element in the civil service and police, in transport and marketing, and were a strong competitor for land in the coastal districts.

The major agricultural and rural development of this period occurred because most of the old German plantations were in the British sector. By 1924, most of these had been sold to the original German owners, a situation which remained until the Second World War. At the beginning of the war these properties were confiscated by the government and in 1946 they were unified and placed under the control of a government entity, the Cameroon Development Corporation. There has been a continual change in the origin of the labour supply for the plantations, in part related to political considerations. In the era of German rule, workers came from all parts of Cameroon, but especially from the Bamenda and Yaoundé areas. After the division of the area into British and French mandates, the number of labourers from the French area declined rapidly, but there was an increase from British-controlled areas, including Nigeria. The granting of independence and the reunification of Cameroon, resulted in the Nigerian source ending almost completely; in fact, in 1962 most Nigerian workers were declared redundant.

It is difficult to make a full assessment and evaluation of the role of the Cameroon Development Corporation in the economy of the Republic of Cameroon, for no authoritative study of this question has yet been published. However, there are some indications that the corporation's contribution has been positive. The construction of numerous roads, the building and staffing of schools, the paying of numerous scholarships for training in engineering, business, and medical skills, and the provision of medical care for a large proportion of the inhabitants of the South Western Province are examples of the indirect contributions the plantations have made for many years. In a more direct manner, the corporation's exports represent a contribution to the economy.

In spite of these possible benefits from the plantation experience, the results for rural development may be viewed as negative. Large-scale migration for long periods of time from the rural areas weakens rural structures and has a negative effect upon agriculture. Employment as a labourer on a plantation is not conducive to the overall development of a self-sufficient class of small farmers, either as individuals or in cooperative efforts. The existence of the plantations, especially in the post-Second World War era, meant that a large proportion of whatever funds were available for this largely neglected territory went to the plantations, and not to agricultural extension, food crop research or infrastructural development outside the plantation area. Indeed, it was only in the mid-1950s that a motor road was extended beyond the town of Bamenda into the heart of the North West Province; that road remains to this day unpaved and for much of its length it is a mere track.

This is not to say that the British colonial administration did absolutely nothing for rural area development. However, most of what was done outside the plantations in this respect was aimed at the encouragement of the growth of export crops, especially cocoa and coffee, and even here, most of what was accomplished was due to African rather than European initiative.

Plantations and cooperatives were two major involvements of the British colonial régime in the rural development of Cameroon. Both of these efforts were aimed at the production of export crops to supply the needs of the industrial states of Western Europe, especially Germany in the interwar period and Britain in the post-Second World War years. Little or no attention was paid to improvements in agricultural technology for local needs, to infrastructural development, or to the formation of integrated, developmental economic structures either within Southern Cameroons or between Southern Cameroons and Nigeria.

Francophone Cameroon

In French Cameroon colonial officials and French settlers had a somewhat different view of the purposes and future of the territory they controlled, but in important respects the results were not greatly different. Although the mandate/trust status was the cause of uneasiness about the long-range disposition of the territory and some large-scale projects were never undertaken on this account, there was, in general, a more positive view of the territory than that held by the British. This resulted in greater private and public investment by France and in a much greater involvement by French citizens in the territory than was to occur in the British areas.

French efforts were high concentrated in a region served by the largely German-built railroad, a 'fertile crescent' extending from Foumban to Douala to Kribi and to Yaoundé. Here were the major urban-industrial centres and the most important agricultural regions, producing coffee, cocoa, tea, palm products and timber. It was in this region that the majority of French citizens settled, often in competition with Cameroon farmers in the production of cash crops.

French efforts concentrated on the expansion of cash crop production, especially cocoa for African planters and coffee and bananas for Europeans. Africans entered coffee production only after the Second World War. A second emphasis through most of the period of French rule was on the development of a small, landed class of wealthy chiefs who, it was thought, would become a strong conservative element in favour of the retention of close ties with the French. Such 'chiefs', who often had no claim to such a title under African law or custom, were created by the French as the major local element in a system of colonial rule.

In similar fashion, the French attempted to promote cocoa growing, the major agricultural innovation for the bulk of the population, in a manner that would encourage the growth of a plantation class of farmers who would be supportive of French colonial rule.

Again, as in the British territory, we see that the major effort of the French in Cameroon development was aimed at the production of export crops and, to some extent, this was to the benefit of expatriate farmers. Little was done to foster the development of food crop production beyond the provision of extension-type services to a limited number of government appointed chiefs. In addition, little concern was shown or action taken on behalf of some sort of integrated Cameroon economic system. The needs of France were predominant in the decision making process that controlled development in French Cameroon.

Another aspect of French rule should be noted, namely, a tendency to plan large-scale, multipurpose projects for rural development which were originated with little or no participation of the rural population in the planning and with little under-standing of the dynamics of Cameroon rural life, or even the great variety that occurs between rural areas of Cameroon.

Rural development and the Republic of Cameroon

In recent years the RC has begun to view agricultural develop-ment as the keystone of overall economic development for the country. Food crops, industrial crops, animal and fish husbandry and forest production are all to be modernized, restructured and revolutionized in an effort to increase production, productivity and the attractiveness of rural living. Cameroon is planning to have a 'Green Revolution'.

President Ahidjo, on the occasion of the Agricultural Show in Buea in 1973, declared that the country was to embark on a Green Revolution, 'to deploy all means capable of promoting the development of the potential of Cameroon's rural production by eliminating anachronistic forms of constraint for the small holder and by creating conditions for a modern agricultural economy.' This transformation requires the introduction of new technology and skills, the alteration of rural structures and the marketing system and the improvement of rural living conditions. In so doing, production and productivity will increase, dependence on a small number of income-producing crops will cease, export earnings will increase and food imports will decrease, nutrition levels will rise, and the rural exodus of youth to the urban centres will be slowed. 'The obligatory modernization of the traditional sector consequently makes it necessary for there to be major changes at the human, technical and economic levels. . . . This policy involves projects connected with production, marketing and the standard of living in the rural areas.'

Like many colonially-imposed rural development plans, there appears to be an assumption that the rural dweller has only his or her labour to contribute to rural development. Rural interests, variances from one rural area to another and rural initiatives and leadership are not a part of the planning for rural development. Thus, we find the continuation of a pattern that arose in 1880s with German colonial policies and the development of a plantation system, that continues through the French colonial period, and now emerges as predominant in the independence era.

A second pattern originating in the colonial era is largely continued in the Green Revolution. Although there is some consideration in the plans for increased food production, particularly in an effort to provide food for the wage-employed class in the urban areas at a low price, emphasis has been devoted to cash crops for export, mainly to Europe. In respect of food, the main consideration is to provide sufficient food, at low prices, for the urban dweller. There is only slight attention paid to the potential role of Cameroon as a supplier of food, such as yams, rice and plantains to its food-deficit neighbours. Also, the emphasis on low food prices for urban dwellers runs contrary to both the food export potential and to the real needs of the rural inhabitant. Food exports are discouraged in order to prevent food shortages in Cameroon urban areas. Food shortages would lead to price rises and price rises would cause urban discontent and problems for the government. Major emphasis in agricultural development continues to be exerted in those crops that supply the European market, rather than food crops for the African market.

As a result, at least in part, of these policies, incomes remain low for the vast majority of rural inhabitants. Rural farmers, however, are not organized, and in most instances probably do not realize what might be gained through organization. Their ability to exert pressure upon government is limited, and any local disturbances are strongly repressed by the police and the military. Rural incomes remain low, and the only means of expressing rural discontent is through migration to urban centres.

Cameroon has a good potential for agricultural growth and development. Available arable land, a lack of population pressure and several food deficit neighbours all suggest an important and profitable role as food supplier to West and Central Africa. The adaptation to such a role requires appropriate planning, decision-making procedures, and follow through on the part of individual farmers, local authorities and the central government. Yet, the history of rural and agricultural development in the past one hundred years has established patterns and practices that inhibit progress towards such an adaptation.

The political process

It is necessary to consider the mode of operation of the Cameroon government and the process whereby the present political system has evolved in order to understand the dimensions of the lack of communication between the rural peasantry and the central government and the almost total lack of participation of those rural masses in that government.

The Ahidjo régime was established in the late 1950s as a direct result of the policies of the French colonial administration. The conservative regime of Ahmadou Ahidjo was installed in power as the independent government of the country in an effort to prevent the more nationalist, left-wing party, the Union des Populations du Cameroun (UPC), from taking power. The electoral process was used by the French administration to put Ahidjo and the Union Camerounaise into office, while the courts, the police and the army were used to destroy the real nationalist party and its leadership. This conflict continued for a long period of time, and the country became independent while a state of war existed.

The effects of this traumatic coming to power (as well as the lessons of events elsewhere in African politics) created a régime which was strongly fearful of opposition. Established in an environment of war and fear, the government remained extremely suspicious of opposition or criticism. The results were a highly centralized administraton in a unitary state, a single party dominated by a few political personalities, and a stern, semi-police state where human rights were often deferred in preference to the survival of the régime.

Yaoundé, the capital of Cameroon, has in recent years become the sole source of administrative decision-making in the country. Local and municipal governments, primary and secondary schools, and loans for agricultural development are only a few of the many tasks that are Yaoundé based. The primary school teacher in Garoua travels to Yaoundé to ask about a promotion and the Chairman of the Young Farmers Club in Mokunda travels to Yaoundé to secure an agricultural loan. The process of the transfer of decision making to the centre, well-advanced in the francophone areas at the time of independence, was continued by the Ahidjo administration. There are no longer any local centres of decision-making. Much like the system that prevails in France, but extended to more intimate detail, local authorities are appointed from Yaoundé, and these officials look to Yaoundé for guidance, promotion, and transfer. This centralization was largely unknown in the anglophone section of the country at the time of reunification, but with the disappearance of the government of the State of West Cameroon when the federation ended in 1972 the full brunt of the centralization process has been brought to bear on the English-speaking parts of the country. The ending of the federation was a major step in breaking up not only an administrative but also a political competitor of Yaoundé, for the old anglophone state with its focus, both administrative and political, on its capital of Buea was now divided into two provinces, each tied directly to Yaoundé. In this case of divide and rule it is no surprise that each of these provinces represents a long-standing competitive group within the anglophone area.

Parallel to the ending of the federation has been the move to end political party pluralism, first in the francophone region and then in the entire country. Numerous tactics were used in this process, including cooptation of the leaders of patron-client parties and force. The overall effect was to develop an organization of patrons at the centre with each tied to his or her client group. Thus, the Cameroon National Union was not a mass party, and it did not serve as a means of communication, participation or mobilization for more than a small group of persons.

To buttress this bureaucratic régime, the government relied on a number of laws – and thus on the police – to stifle that opposition which could not be coopted or coerced. Jean-François Bayart, in 'One-party government and political development in Cameroon' *African Affairs* no. 72 (April 1973, p. 125–44), argues that the predominant ideology of the Ahidjo government was the 'ethic of unity' which aimed at the dissolution of all loyalties except loyalty to the nation. In order to implement this ethic, Cameroon law, according to Bayart provides for the arrest of 'whosoever shall give utterance to or propagate false reports, news or rumours, or tenditious commentaries on accurate news when such news, rumour or commentary may tend to be damaging of the public authorities. . . .' Persons were arrested and held for political reasons and newspapers were subjected to administrative censorship prior to final printing. Several books on Cameroon politics were banned.

In its effort to promote the 'ethic of unity' the government attempted to destroy possible alternative foci of loyalty. It was not only pluralistic party systems and the Federal Republic that were to be eliminated, but other types of organizations disappeared or became attached to government or party structures. Thus, trade unions, youth and women's groups lost their independent existence.

So there arose a government that was cut off from the public, a public that could not communicate with its government. Bayart is correct when he writes that 'The white-collar workers, manual workers, and peasants for their part no longer [had] available specific channels through which to express their demands . . . the farmers can put forward their interests only when administrative tours take place; prefects and subprefects have become their sole representatives,' see Jean-François Bayart's 'Les catégories dirigeantes au Cameroon' in *Revue Francais d'Etudes Politiques Africaines*, no. 105 (Sept. 1974). The bureaucracy became the predominant force after the President and his small group of top party officials. It is by satisfying the needs of these groups (and their military counterparts) that the political élite stayed in power. Only minimal attention needed to be paid to the majority of the population.

President Ahidjo, the designer and builder of the political system just described, resigned in 1982, turning most powers over to his designated replacement, Paul Biya. It appears that Biya's intention has been to assert firm control of the political system and to move it towards a more democratic process. Unfortunately, the requirements of the first goal have made it difficult to progress toward the second goal.

Such progress might have been more rapid and concrete if ex-President Ahidjo had fully relinquished power and if he had been content to remain in retirement. However, this was not the case. Ahidjo apparently believed that he could safely put Biya in the presidency, but real power would remain with Ahidjo. The former president had trained and groomed Biya and felt that his client would remain obedient. Also, Ahidjo retained the presidency of the only political party and he appointed Biya's first cabinet. But, Biya proved to be quite independent, the party voted Ahidjo out of office, and Biya dismantled the Ahidjo cabinet. As these events took place, Biya also took steps to restore the freedom of the press, to quell the secret police, and there was talk of reforming the electoral and party systems: the machinery for repression was turned off but not dismantled. This movement towards democracy was crushed in April 1984 when a serious *coup d'état* was attempted in Ahidjo's favour. The immediate needs of security led to the reopening of a period of repression, a period that may be shortlived and will end as the real threat of further violence subsides.

Cameroon is a country with true promise for economic growth and development. Political stability has existed for most of its independent history and there is some hope for the development of a more democratic political process. The outlook for the future of this African country remains positive.

The bibliography

This volume in the World Bibliographical Series has been prepared to serve the needs of the general reader. The references included were selected on the basis of their individual significance in the total body of literature on Cameroon, but also with respect to their availability to the public. That body of literature exists mainly in three languages, German, French and English, which are the languages of the colonial occupiers of Cameroon. However, we have stressed the English-language materials in our selection process.

This is not a comprehensive bibliography, for its primary purpose is to serve the reader who needs a quick introduction to the major works on Cameroon. However, sufficient information is provided here for those who need in-depth knowledge of any aspect of Cameroon studies to begin their research. Careful use of the bibliography chapter of this volume and attention to the individual references throughout the volume (which note each item containing a singificant bibliography) will guide the scholar to the full extent of Camerooniana.

Introduction

The items referenced here include an annotation, generally a brief description of the work or, in the case of edited volumes, a summary of the table of contents. At the end of each chapter there is a list of cross-references to relevant items in other chapters.

Acknowledgements

It is an impossible task to list all of those persons who aided and encouraged us in the preparation of this volume, for in a strong sense this effort has drawn upon our experience in Cameroon studies since 1967. In Cameroon, we must note Drs. Martin Njeuma and Simon-Joseph Epale, two of the most helpful of scholars. In the United States, numerous members of the staff of the Cooper Library at the University of South Carolina and graduate assistants from the Department of Government and International Studies have aided us. In particular, we wish to thank Mr. Dan Boice, Director of the Interlibrary Loan Office and his predecessors, David Stoelting and Taifa Yu.

In an earlier period, the staffs of the old reading room of the International African Institute and the Library of the School of Oriental and African Studies were of special assistance. Our special gratitude is extended to Lori S. Joyce who with great patience and humour typed the manuscript – in spite of the compilers' lack of organizational skills and handwriting.

The Country and Its People

1 **L'Année Politique et Économique Africaine.** (The African Political and Economic Year.)
Dakar: Société Africaine d'Edition, 1964-. annual.
This publication is a valuable source of information on twenty-six separate African nations, including Cameroon. Each nation is discussed individually in terms of salient political and economic occurrences for a given year. Especially useful is the wealth of statistics pertaining to various sectors of the national economy.

2 **Cameroon: forward with confidence.**
AfricaAsia, no. 7 (July 1984), 44p.
This special edition on Cameroon contains brief essays on politics, the press, music, foreign policy, transport, power, agriculture, sport, and education. Although the journal generally presents a sceptical view of Cameroon politics and economics, this issue was quite favourable to the Biya régime. *AfricaAsia* (or *Afriqueasie*) is a good source of current commentary on Cameroon society.

3 **L'Encyclopédie de la République Unie du Cameroun.** (Encyclopaedia of the United Republic of Cameroon.)
Abidjan, Dakar, Lomé: Nouvelles Editions Africaines, 1981. 4 vols.
The titles of the four volumes are: vol. 1, 'The physical context and the people'; vol. 2, 'History and the state'; vol. 3, 'The economy'; and vol. 4, 'The life of the nation'.

1

4 **Le Cameroun.** (Cameroon.)
Jean Imbert. Paris: Presses Universitaires de France, 1982. 128p. 4
maps. bibliog.

This book is one of the popular general French series entitled *Que Sais-je?* It is
useful for quick reference as well as providing the reader with a comprehensive
overview of the subject examined. The geography, history, political structures and
processes, social and cultural evolution, and economic development of Cameroon
are outlined in this volume. Concise writing is matched with important data to
provide the newcomer to Cameroon studies or the interested traveller with an
overview of the country.

5 **Know your country: know Cameroon.**
Paris: Afrique Biblio Club, 1979. 78p. 3 maps.

This general overview of Cameroon is unique in that it is presented in cartoon
form utilizing colour drawings. Each general issue discussed is presented with two
pages of cartoon depictions with short descriptions and two pages of text
highlighting its salient features. Topics discussed include Cameroon history,
political party and government structures, geography, the diversity of ethnic
groups, agriculture, industry, travel, cities, music, and scientific and technical
research. The work is useful in that it presents the key aspects of Cameroon in a
highly simplified yet encompassing manner. This is a government-sanctioned view
of Cameroon history.

6 **Africa Contemporary Record: Annual Survey and Documents.**
Edited by Colin Legum. London: Rex Collings; New York: Holmes
& Meier, 1968- . annual.

Each edition contains an essay on Cameroon as well as general studies of African
politics and economics. This is also a valuable source for statistical data.

7 **Cameroun.** (Cameroon.)
B. Lembezat. Paris: Nouvelles Editions Latines, 1964. 154p. map.
bibliog.

One of a general collection entitled *Surval du Monde*, the present volume
provides a handy sized general reference guide to Cameroon. Informative sections
describe the geography, history, economy, political evolution, and salient aspects
of the post-independence Ahidjo régime.

8 **Area handbook for the United Republic of Cameroon.**
Harold D. Nelson, Margarita Dobert (*et al.*). Washington, DC: US
Government Printing Office, 1974. 335p. 11 maps. bibliog.

This area handbook series is an excellent starting point for research on any
country included in the series. A multidisciplinary, non-technical approach makes
this volume useful at any level of interest. The titles of the main sections are
'Social,' 'Political,' 'Economic,' and 'National security.' However, information on
ethnography, demography, the arts, education and other subjects is also included.
There is an extensive bibliography, a useful index, and a brief glossary.

Du Cameroun au Hoggar. (From Cameroon to Hoggar.)
See item no. 18.

African clearings.
See item no. 120.

Le Cameroun: les indigènes, les colons, les missions, l'administration Française. (Cameroon: natives, settlers, missions, French administration.)
See item no. 144.

Black sheep, adventures in West Africa.
See item no. 178.

Le Cameroun. (Cameroon.)
See item no. 271.

Geography

9 **Le Cameroun fédéral.** (Federal Cameroon.)
Pierre Billard.   Lyons, France: Tixier & Fils, 1968. 2 vols. map.
bibliog.

The first volume of this set is an examination of the 'physical' geography of
Cameroon. Subjects discussed in depth are flora and fauna, hydrography,
climates, and relief structures. The second volume deals with the 'human' and
'economic' geography of Cameroon. The section on economic geography focuses
on mineral resources, agriculture and fishing, transportation, the infrastructure,
industry, the economy, and tourism. Human geography is discussed in chapters
centering on the indigenous populations, political processes, and social action.

10 **Géographie du Cameroun.** (Geography of Cameroon.)
Centre d'Edition et de Production pour l'Enseignement et la
Recherche.   Yaoundé: Centre d'Edition et de Production pour
l'Enseignement et la Recherche, 1978. 287p. 26 maps.

This is a standard French secondary school textbook utilized in Cameroon. The
text is built around four topical areas of study: physical geography, the human
'milieu' and development, the national economy, and economic regions. The text
is complemented by an array of charts, photographs, and pictures and also
includes resumés of each chapter and an extensive glossary of terms.

11 **Atlas régional ouest I.** (Regional atlas, west.)
Georges Courade.   Yaoundé: ORSTOM, [n.d.], 266p. 6 maps.
bibliog.

This atlas deals specifically with the region of Western Cameroon. After a brief
description of the method of collection and utilization of various data, a detailed
regional analysis is made of the area. Factors examined include the physical
milieu, the various groups which inhabit the region, and the lasting effects of

European penetration. The social and economic organization of individuals and their principal activities are also discussed. Finally, the author presents the development possibilities of this geographical region. This volume is one of a series which is intended to cover the entire country.

12   **Notes on the Cameroon mountain.**
     G. M. D. Guillaume.   Buea, Cameroon: Government Printer,
     1966. 16p. 2 maps. bibliog.
Mount Cameroon, the tallest peak in West Africa, is approximately 13,350 feet high, and twenty-eight miles long, and covers a total area of nearly 700 square miles. The author collected the notes for this booklet while pursuing his hobby of ascending Mount Cameroon.

13   **Atlas of the United Republic of Cameroon.**
     Edited by Georges Laclavère, introduction by Jean-Félix
     Loung.   Paris: Editions Jeune Afrique, 1980. 72p. 33 maps.
This is one of a series of African atlases first published by Jeune Afrique in 1973. Each chapter is built around a thematic concept (such as geology, climate, racial groups and languages) and is comprised of two distinct elements. Each chapter begins with an extremely detailed colour map so as to visually present the topic. This is followed by a concise commentary which explains the content of the map as well as presenting the data from which it was drawn. This atlas is a superb document in that it is very concise and beautifully detailed, while at the same time being highly informative. However, some of the essays are badly out of date and consider only limited aspects of the subject.

14   **A new geography of Cameroon.**
     J. A. Ngwa.   London: Longman, 1978. 151p. 50 maps.
A standard secondary school textbook encompassing twenty chapters, questions and exercises, and fifty maps and diagrams. Major sections include historical knowledge of Cameroon, physical geography, economic development, and aspects of human and social geography. Two final sections provide brief revision for the student and instructional notes for the teachers. The emphasis in this publication is on the anglophone portion of the country, but it remains a useful introduction to Cameroon geography.

The urban development of Buea: an essay in social geography.
See item no. 211.

A political geography of Africa.
See item no. 310.

Cameroon-Central African Republic boundary.
See item no. 319.

Black Africa develops.
See item no. 333.

Geography

Regional policy in Cameroon: the case of planning without facts.
See item no. 344.

Planification économique et projections spatiales au Cameroun. (Economic planning and spatial projections in Cameroon.)
See item no. 345.

Travellers' Accounts

15 **Lords of the Equator: an African journey.**
Patrick Balfour.   London: Hutchinson, 1939. 282p.
This account of the author's travels across the mandated and other territories of
Equatorial Africa presents the perceptions of an individual who went only to
those places which could be reached by motor transport. One section out of the
four which comprise the book describes in detail the author's travels in the
mandated territories of Cameroon. The chapter provides an account of the
peoples and sights which the author encountered in British and French
Cameroon.

16 **Zintgraff's explorations in Bamenda: Adamawa and the Benue lands
1889-1892.**
E. M. Chilver.   Buea, Cameroon: Ministry of Primary Education
and Social Welfare and West Cameroon Antiquities Commission,
1966. 34p. 2 maps. bibliog.
This pamphlet is the second of a general historical series published by the West
Cameroon government concerning the history of Cameroon. The contents are a
collection of brief extracts and summaries from Eugen Zintgraff's book *Nord-
Kamerun*. The sections of the work which are quoted describe Zintgraff's
journeys within the Bamenda territories of Adamawa and the Benue lands.
Zintgraff (1858-97), was a German explorer who ventured into the Lower Congo
and extensively explored Cameroon. Five plates depict various aspects of
Zintgraff's travels.

17 **African majesty: a record of refuge at the court of the King of Bangangté in the French Cameroons.**
F. Clement C. Egerton.   New York: Charles Scribner's Sons, 1939. 348p. map.

The author describes in great detail his travels in French Cameroon in 1938. The first part of the account presents Egerton's sojourn in Ebolowa among the Bulu people on his way to Bangangté. However, most of the volume concentrates on the author's several months study with N'Jike II, the tenth king of Bangangté. The work supplies the reader not only with an historical account of one individual's travels, but also with a factual account of the lives and customs of the Bangangté peoples in the 1930s.

18 **Du Cameroun au Hoggar.** (From Cameroon to Hoggar.)
M. de Lyée de Belleau.   Paris: Editions Alsatia, 1945. 171p.

The author, writing in 1945, defends French colonialism by asserting that it protected Cameroon from German tutelage and contributed to its development. This work is a collection of short essays written in story form which describe the salient aspects and remembrances of the author's travels in Cameroon. The essays are grouped under major headings, such as 'Civilization of southern Cameroon,' and 'British Nigerian territories.' Each individual essay, however, provides a unique insight into certain aspects of the indigenous Cameroonian culture and colonial rule. Examples include 'The mysterious pygmees,' 'The missions of Edea,' 'What are the whites doing here?' and 'On the route of Foumbam.'

19 **Through British Cameroons.**
Frederick William Hugh Migeod.   London: Heath Cranton, 1925. 285p. map.

This is an account of the author's travels through Cameroon in 1928. The trip begins at Victoria and ends at Yola, on the River Benue. These recollections, while providing interesting reading, recreate Cameroon society as it existed in 1928. Highly detailed descriptions are presented of the various day-to-day activities of the many peoples inhabiting the area. The reader is taken on excursions which lead to an ascent of Mount Cameroon, a stop among the peoples of the forest region, an examination of the plantations, and a stay in Munshi country. The text is complemented by many photographs.

20 **A travers le Cameroun du sud au nord: voyages et explorations dans l'arrière-pays de 1889 à 1891.** (Across Cameroon from south to north: voyages and explorations in the back country from 1889 to 1891.)
Curt Von Morgen.   Yaoundé: L'Université Fédéral du Cameroun, 1972. 215p. map.

This translation of a German officer's personal account of his role in the colonization of Cameroon not only gives the reader the biased impressions of a colonial agent as to the 'positive' aspects of colonial imperialism, but also provides historians with a valuable presentation of Cameroon as it existed before the arrival of the European *en masse*. The traditional lives and workings of pre-colonial Cameroon society are richly described. The author portrays events such as 'combats with the Malimba,' 'discovering of the Mbam,' and 'traps of the Bati.' The book is enhanced by dozens of original engravings depicting pre-colonial Cameroon.

Tourist Guides

21 **Cameroon.**
Cameroon. Ministry of Information and Tourism. Yaoundé:
Cameroon, Ministry of Information and Tourism; Paris: Presse
Africaine Associée, 1970. 189p. 2 maps.

Although slightly dated, this is an excellent reference guide and souvenir for all who are interested in acquiring a general knowledge of Cameroon. The first section entitled 'Unity in diversity' describes the history of the various peoples and regions of Cameroon. The second section examines the people and their institutions, focusing on topics such as public health, new roles for women, and the armed forces. The third section covers national resources, industrial development, development planning, and the investment code. The fourth section entitled 'Beautiful Cameroon' highlights the major tourist attractions of the nation. The text is complemented by dozens of colour photos which present various aspects of daily life in Cameroon.

22 **Au Cameroun.** (To Cameroon.)
Alain Camus. Paris: Hachette, 1981. 213p. 9 maps. (Guides
Bleus).

This portable tourist guide provides a brief account of the history, geography, peoples, and present day-to-day living and working conditions of the nation. Special tips for the traveller are included in a section entitled 'De l'usage du Cameroun.' Points of interest, descriptions of minor towns and numerous ethnic groups, hotel accommodation, and other tourist information is presented under four major headings: travel in the north, in the south, in the west, and in Douala.

23 Cameroon today.
Anne Debel.   Paris: Editions J. A., 1977. 255p. 19 maps.
This volume, which is available in English, French, and German editions, is an
ideal tourist guide and souvenir for all who are interested in travel in Cameroon.
The first half of the book is devoted to a panoramic overview of the nation,
stressing the diverse nature of Cameroon life. The second half of the guide is
geared towards travel in Cameroon. Brief summaries are presented concerning
the unique aspects of over thirty towns and sites, with short sections describing
travel arrangements to and within the nation, daily life, sports, food, souvenirs,
accommodation and hotels. The text is complemented by ninety-eight pages of
colour photographs and nineteen maps and plans.

Flora and Fauna

24　**Larger birds of West Africa.**
David A. Bannerman.　Harmondsworth, England: Penguin, 1958.
195p.

This volume contains fifty-four black and white sketches. It includes the birds of anglophone Cameroon, as well as many species in francophone Cameroon. The latter area is more specifically covered in Bannerman's eight-volume work, but the small volume discussed here is perhaps more useful for someone undertaking field-work. While the sketches are accurate, the lack of colour makes identification difficult. The author has studied and taught in West Africa.

25　**West African insects.**
John Boorman.　Harlow, Essex, England: Longman, 1981. 88p.
bibliog. (West African Nature Handbooks).

The author has spent ten years studying insects in West Africa. In this volume he presents non-technical descriptions, drawings, and colour photographs of representatives of each of the major insect groups. This is a valuable book for the non-specialist.

26　**Small mammals of West Africa.**
A. H. Booth.　London: Longmans, Green, 1960. 68p. map. (West African Nature Handbooks).

The whole of Cameroon is included in this volume which contains brief discussions of seventy-six small mammals. A coloured drawing of each is included in twenty plates. Like the other volumes in the Longman, Green West African Nature Handbooks series, this volume is written for the general reader who desires to identify and learn about the fauna in his or her locale.

27 **West African snakes.**
G. S. Cansdale. London: Longmans, Green, 1961. 74p. (West
African Nature Handbooks).

Fifteen colour plates and well-written descriptions of the snakes make this a
useful guide. Five categories of snakes are discussed – pythons, harmless snakes,
back-fanged snakes, cobras and mambas, and vipers. There is also a chapter on
the treatment of snakebite. Personal experience has proven the value of this guide
to the identification of West African snakes, and its compact size makes it
particularly useful.

28 **Birds of the West African town and garden.**
John H. Elgood. London: Longmans, Green, 1960. 66p. (West
African Nature Handbooks).

Twenty plates, each of which include several species accurately depicted in full
colour, and a simple, straight forward presentation make this a useful field guide
for those with little experience of bird-watching. As the title indicates, this is not a
general guide, for it includes only species found in the town and garden.
However, for these locales it provides a quite thorough coverage. Latin and
English names, description, distribution, habits, and call are presented for one
hundred species in thirty-five families. The volume also provides a sketch of each
species. The author studied and taught in West Africa.

29 **West African trees.**
D. Gledhill. Harlow, Essex, England: Longman, 1972. 72p. (West
African Nature Handbooks).

Approximately ninety trees are discussed under the main headings of swamp
forest, evergreen forest, semi-deciduous forest, riverine forest, secondary forest,
savanna, and 'introduced' trees. Black and white and colour sketches are
provided to aid in the identification of species. English, Latin and some African
names are given, and the volume also contains a useful index. The author, who is
an English university professor, spent several years in West Africa.

30 **The birds of French Cameroon.**
A. I. Good. Yaoundé: L'Institut Français d'Afrique Noire, Centre
du Cameroun, 1952. 203p. Reprinted 1953. 269p. (Sciences
Naturelles, nos. 2 and 3).

The author is one of the most knowledgeable specialists on the subject of
Cameroon ornithology. This two volume set describes in detail over 748 types of
birds that can be found in the former French Cameroon. Several of the listings
include a physical description of the bird in question and its general habitat. An
appendix in volume two lists 183 types of birds which are 'likely' to be found in
French Cameroon. Three extensive indexes arranged alphabetically include the
French, English, and scientific names of each bird listed.

Flora and Fauna

31   **Large mammals of West Africa.**
     D. C. D. Happold.   London: Longman, 1973. 105p. map. bibliog.
     (West African Nature Handbooks).

The larger mammals of West Africa, and some of the smaller mammals which are
not included in the companion volume by A. H. Booth, *Small mammals of West
Africa* (q.v.), are described in the first half of this publication. Colour or
black and white photographs are provided for most species. The second half of
the book discusses West African game preserves, listing facilities available, open
dates, access, special features, species present, and useful data. For Cameroon,
the Bénoué, Boubandjidah, Waza, Kimbe River, and Mbi Crater reserves and
parks are included. This handbook and the others in the Longman series have
been proven by use in the field to be excellent sources.

32   **West African freshwater fish.**
     Michael Holden, William Reed.   London: Longman, 1972. 68p.
     bibliog. (West African Nature Handbooks).

About eighty freshwater fish are described and illustrated in this volume, which is
intended for the non-expert. The examples are drawn from the Niger-Benue
system, but the same fish are to be found everywhere in West Africa, including
Cameroon. Fish from specialized habitats are not included. A chapter on
traditional fishing gear and methods is included.

33   **Flore du Cameroun. Vol. 1. Introduction phytogéographique.** (Flora
     of Cameroon. Vol. 1. Phytogeographical introduction.)
     R. Letouzey.   Paris: Musée Nationale d'Histoire Naturelle, 1963.
     174p. maps.

This is the first of several volumes in a series on Cameroon flora. In 1968, eight
volumes, under the general editorship of André Aubreville, had been published.

34   **The grassland vegetation of the Cameroons mountain.**
     T. D. Maitland.   *Kew Bulletin*, vol. 9 (1932), p. 417-25.

Mount Cameroon, the highest mountain in West Africa, is the predominant
physical structure of the coastal area of Cameroon. Its vegetation is both
grassland and forest.

35   **L'Evolution actuelle des milieux naturels au Cameroun central et
     occidental.** (The present evolution of natural environments in
     Central and West Cameroon.)
     S. Morin.   *Travaux de l'Institut de Géographie de Reims*, nos. 45-46
     (1981), p. 117-39.

Habitat evolution may be influenced by rural and urban planning – or the lack of
it. In this article, Morin predicts some of the effects in the Cameroon situation.

36 **Ecological notes on West African vegetation: the upland forests of Cameroons mountain.**
P. W. Richards. *Journal of Ecology*, vol. 51, no. 3 (1963), p. 529-54.

The huge Mt. Cameroon covers a large proportion of the anglophone coastal province. The forests on the mountain retain many of the characteristics of a virgin forest.

The overloaded ark.
See item no. 434.

The Bafut beagles.
See item no. 435.

A zoo in my luggage.
See item no. 436.

The new Noah.
See item no. 437.

Peoples

37 **In French Cameroons, Bandjoon.**
A. Albert, translated by John Mary.   Ottawa: Les Editions de
l'Arbre, 1943. 340p. map.

This study is the result of the author's ten years of missionary work among the
Bamileke of Bandjoon. As both anthropologist and missionary, Father Albert
produces an account of the beliefs, customs, and social structure of the
'Bandjooners.' The first two chapters explain how the concept of a 'supreme
being' has disappeared from the minds of the Bandjooners because of the role of
the chief who is considered both 'king' and 'god,' and because of the 'totalitarian'
structure of the Bandjoon society. The rest of the work describes Bandjoon
society, rules of organization, justice and law, war, magic, and proverbs and
legends. As in many studies prepared by missionaries, polygamy is a major topic.

38 **Le groupe dit Pahouin (Fang-Boulou-Beti).** (The group called
Pahouin (Fang-Boulou-Beti).)
Pierre Alexandre, Jacques Binet.   Paris: Presses Universitaires de
France, 1958. 152p. bibliog. (Monographies Ethnologiques
Africaines).

One of a series of ethnographical studies of African peoples produced under the
direction of the International African Institute of London, this work examines the
Pahouin peoples of North Western Cameroon. The first two chapters outline the
Pahouin peoples in terms of geography, climate, ethnicity, and history. Chapters
three and four provide a brief summary of the Pahouin languages and economic
life. The majority of the work, however, is devoted to an analysis of the social
organization, principal cultural elements, and general evolution of the Pahouin
peoples. An extensive bibliography of relevant materials is included.

39 **Coastal Bantu of the Cameroons.**
   Edwin Ardener, foreword by Daryll Forde. London: International
   African Institute, 1956. 116p. 2 maps. bibliog. (Western Africa,
   Part II).

This study forms a part of the 'Ethnographic Survey of Africa' prepared under the direction of the International African Institute. The volume is an extensive presentation of the coastal Bantu peoples of Cameroon, and it examines such topics as ethnic groupings, language, social organization, and religious beliefs and culture. The richness of the study is complemented by detailed charts and tables of genealogy, vocabulary, and kinship structure and terminology. The report is based on the personal research of the author and on a thorough survey of the literature.

40 **The history and social institutions of the Ngemba chiefdoms of
   Mbatu, Akum, Nsongwa, Chomba and Ndzong.**
   Pius Soh Bejeng. Yaoundé: ONAREST, [n.d.]. 95p. map.
   (Travaux et Documents de l'Institut des Sciences Humaines, no. 9).

Rather than emphasize the larger kingdoms of the Bamenda plateau (namely, Bali, Mankon, and Bafut), the author presents the first study of the smaller Bamenda plateau kingdoms of Mbatu, Akum, Nsongwa, Chomba, and Ndzong. Each kingdom is examined separately in terms of its geography, general history, social customs, political structures, and economic situation.

41 **Friends and twins in Bangwa.**
   Robert Brain. In: *Man in Africa*. Edited by Mary Douglas, Phyllis
   M. Kaberry. Garden City, New York: Anchor Books, 1971, p.
   214-28.

The Bangwa are one of several groups within the broad category of Bamileke people of the central highlands of Cameroon. Most of the Bamileke chiefdoms are in the francophone part of the country; Bangwa is in the anglophone sector. Here, Robert Brain, an expert on Bangwa society, discusses concepts of friendship, equality between humans, and twins – 'the only true equals, and therefore the best friends' (p. 216) in Bangwa culture. The author demonstrates how these beliefs about the meaning of friendship have assisted the Bangwa in the modern economy of Cameroon, enabling young men to join together in farming, saving money, building houses, and in recreation.

42 **Bangwa kinship and marriage.**
   Robert Brain. Cambridge, England: Cambridge University Press,
   1972. 195p. map. bibliog.

This is a thorough analysis of the Bangwa kinship system, marking an important contribution to Bamileke studies. The nine Bangwa chiefdoms are examined in terms of the ways in which political, economic, and kinship ties bind together a small community. The topics discussed include the Bangwa double descent system, interpersonalities of kinship, and relations of affinity and alliance as a result of marriage. The Bangwa are the only Bamileke society located in anglophone Cameroon.

17

43 **Racial classification and identity in the Meiganga region, North Cameroon.**
Philip Burnham. In: *Race*. Edited by Paul Baxter, Basil Sansom. Harmondsworth, England: Penguin, 1972, p. 301-18.

Burnham examines the past and present significance of racial categories in the ethnically and racially plural society of Meiganga, an administrative district of the Adamawa region of Northern Cameroon. An introductory section describes race and ethnicity in Meiganga. Other topics discussed are the structural basis of Mbororo racial attitudes, the historical basis of Fulbe racial heterogeneity, race and social mobility in post-colonial Fulbe society, and the reasons for the persistence of Fulbe racial attitudes.

44 **Opportunity and constraint in a savanna society: the Gbaya of Meiganga, Cameroon.**
Philip Burnham. London, New York: Academic Press, 1980. 324p. 3 maps. bibliog.

This work is the result of ten years of study of the Gbaya people. The 'fluidity' of Gbaya social structure within an economic system that enjoys structural independence from the national economy of Cameroon is described. Ethnicity, rather than age, rank, or social class, is the designated factor by which life within the Meiganga sub-prefecture assumes political meaning. The author's goal is to present a theory of Gbaya social change which counters 'general explanations' of change, preferring instead long-term individual empirical studies at the local level.

45 **Population du Moyen Logone: Tchad et Cameroun.** (Population of the Middle Logone: Chad and Cameroon.)
Jean Cabot, Roland Dizian, preface by Gouverneur Hubert Deschamps. Paris: ORSTOM, 1955. 12 maps. bibliog. (L'Homme d'Outre-mer, no.1).

This is a study of the Mayo-Kebbi peoples of Chad and the Diamare peoples of Chad and Cameroon who share a common transnational environment entitled Moyen Logone (Middle Logone). The first half of the study, conducted by Jean Cabot, describes ethnic aspects of the Mayo-Kebbi peoples and the specific projects which can be instituted to improve the land and living conditions in the Moyen Logone. The second half of the study, conducted by Roland Dizian, presents the geographic, ethnic, and demographic traits of Cameroon's Diamare peoples situated within the Moyen Logone. For a more recent and more general survey of Northern populations, refer to G. Pontie and J. Boutrais, 'Les sociétés' in *Le nord du Cameroun: des hommes, une region* (Paris: ORSTOM, 1984), p. 203-304.

46 **Traditional Bamenda: the pre-colonial history and ethnography of the Bamenda grassfields.**
E. M. Chilver, P. M. Kaberry. Buea, Cameroon: Ministry of Primary Education and Social Welfare and West Cameroon Antiquities Commission, 1967. 134p. map.

In this history of the pre-colonial Bamenda peoples of Western Cameroon, the rst four chapters discuss the language distribution and geography of these rassland peoples, as well as the evidence of early settlement and peopling of the rea. The majority of the book is devoted to the traditions of migration, the ettlement, and state formation of Bamenda, with selected examples of social and olitical institutions being presented for individual chiefdoms (namely, Tadkon, Igie, and Fungom). Also discussed is the traditional Bamenda agricultural conomy and material culture.

7 **Ritual, conflict, and meaning in an African society.**
   Richard G. Dillon. *Ethos*, vol. 5, no. 2 (Summer 1977), p. 151-73. bibliog.

he author compares and contrasts the explanatory appropriateness of traditional funtionalist,' more modern 'political,' and alternative 'intellectualist' approaches o explaining a Meta ritual of curing and conflict resolution. After briefly escribing Meta culture and society, a diviner's diagnosis of one case and the ubsequent ritual enacted are discussed. The three above stated approaches are xamined in the light of the ritual, and the author concludes that the alternative ntellectual approach embodies the greatest explanatory power. The Meta's upernatural concepts are said to comprise a 'theoretical idiom' through which omplex problems involving illness, infertility, and disturbed social relations can e understood. Once understood, the ritual provides a setting in which problems an be addressed and treated.

8 **Violent conflict in Meta society.**
   Richard G. Dillon. *American Ethnologist*, vol. 7, no. 4 (Nov. 1980), p. 658-73. bibliog.

he author points out the weaknesses of the 'social structural' approach to violent onflict and suggests ways to overcome them. Social structuralists, for example, re said to rely on over simplistic models describing the relationship between iolence and social violence and have ignored 'cultural mechanisms' which can nfluence the management of violence. Four separate cases of conflict in Meta ociety are presented to show the inadequacy of the social structural approach.

9 **Inventaire ethnique du Sud-Cameroun.** (Ethnic inventory of South Cameroon.)
   Idelette Dugast. Yaoundé: l'Institut Français d'Afrique Noire, 1949. 159p. 60 maps. bibliog. (Populations, no. 1).

This ethnographic survey provides a detailed analysis of the various peoples who nhabit francophone Southern Cameroon. Each chapter concentrates on a single thnic grouping (such as the Duala), and subsequently divides these into the ifferent peoples who make up this grouping (such as the Pongo, Wuri, and 3odiman). The author provides a brief overview of each major grouping, fterwards examining in greater detail the specific characteristics of the peoples of vhich it is composed. Characteristics discussed include physical and human eography, language, and anthropological demography. Also included are inguistic, anthropological, and general bibliographies.

19

50   **Monographie de la tribu des Ndiki (Banen du Cameroun).**
     (Monograph on the Ndiki tribe (the Banen of Cameroon).)
     Idelette Dugast.   Paris: Institut d'Ethnologie, 1959. 633p. 3 maps.
     bibliog.

This is the second of two volumes which examine the Ndiki people (a sub
grouping of the overall Banen peoples) of South Western Cameroon. The fir
volume of the set presents the material life of the Ndiki, while this volum
examines their social and family lives. The documentation is extensive in that it
the result of field research which was carried out in the area between 1934 an
1956. The first part of the study situates the Ndiki people socially, historicall
and geographically. The rest of the book is divided into three major subheading
psychological underpinnings, the family, and social goods of the individual an
society. Two extensive annexes document the language and divination practices
the Banen.

51   **Aspects of the life style and culture of women in the Fulbe districts o
     Maroua.**
     Miriam Joy Eguchi.   *Kyoto University African Studies*, vol. 8
     (1973), p. 17-92.

Although Maroua 'has not reached the level of Europeanization found in larg
cities such as Yaoundé,' it provides an excellent example of how 'materi
progress and town living bring about social and cultural change.' Topics discusse
include housing, dress, hygiene, the housewife, food preparation, earning mone
marriage, sex life, childbirth and infant care, music, magic, health, and educatior

52   **The tradition of a people: Bakossi.**
     S. N. Ejedepang-Koge, foreword by Engelbert Mveng.   Yaoundé:
     the author, 1971. 354p. 8 maps. bibliog.

This study is the result of eleven years of research and fieldwork by the autho
who is a member of the Bakossi people. Ejedepang-Koge, who organized and wa
president of the 'mwan'Ngoe Youth movement,' initiated this study in order t
preserve and reinvigorate 'the dying tradition of Bakossi.' The major sections o
the book cover the geographic environment, historical setting, institution
material culture, and linguistic background of the Bakossi. Each major section
highly detailed and divided into various sub-sections. The section concernin
'institutions,' for example, examines marriage, birth, circumcision, omens
death, rites, juju societies, forces of peace and order, land ownership, and lineag
systems. As stated in the preface, the book is special in that it represents th
author's discovery, 'through his personal experience, of his own tribal and cultura
heritage.'

53   **Tradition and change in peasant activities: a study of the indigenous
     people's search for cash in the South-West Province of Cameroon.**
     S. N. Ejedepang-Koge.   Yaoundé: the author, 1975. 328p. 4 maps
     bibliog.

The primary purpose of the study is to elucidate how traditional and moder
methods of earning a living interact or conflict with an individual's search fo

immediate happiness in the present world. More precisely, the study discusses the peasantry's search for cash. The first section analyses the physical and human factors influencing peasant activities. The second section discusses the forms and mechanisms and the struggle to earn cash in the cash economy. The third section comprises regional studies which consider economic zones of the South-West Province, bringing out their special characteristics, successes, potentialities, and problems. General conclusions are drawn.

4 **Les Massa du Cameroun: vie économique et sociale.** (The Massa of
   Cameroon: economic and social life.)
   Igor de Garine.   Paris: Presses Universitaires de France, 1964.
   250p. 16 maps. bibliog. (Etudes Ethnographiques).
In this ethnographical study of the Massa people of Northern Cameroon the author argues that contemporary Massa society has been influenced by three separate forces: neighbouring populations, Islamic kingdoms and their tributaries, and European colonialism. The first section examines the geography, history, material culture, and community of the Massa. The second section examines the economic life of the Massa, centering on concepts such as production techniques, commerce, and family budgets. The final section describes social organization and the traditional distribution of societal goods.

5 **Les Fali Hou et Tsalo: montagnards du Nord-Cameroun.** (The Fali
   Hou and Tsalo: highlanders of North Cameroon.)
   J. G. Gauthier.   Oosterhout, Netherlands: Anthropological
   Publications, 1969. 272p. bibliog.
The author conducted extensive field research over an eight-year period, which resulted in this study which centres on the mountain dwelling Hou and Tsalo Fali of Northern Cameroon. Broad generalizations are derived from a specific study of the Fali of Ngoutchoumi. The material life of the Fali is examined in terms of their physical and human milieu, history and migration patterns, and economic life and techniques. Other sections of the book shed light on Fali social and political structures, social life, and specific cultural elements. Also see this author's essay in *Contribution de la recherche ethnologique à l'histoire des civilisations du Cameroun*, vol. 1. (Paris: CNRS, 1981.), edited by C. Tandits.

6 **Spider divination in the Cameroons.**
   Paul Gebauer.   Milwaukee, Wisconsin: Milwaukee Public
   Museum, 1964. 157p. 4 maps. bibliog. (Publications in
   Anthropology, no. 10).
Spider divination is a practice performed throughout sub-Saharan Africa. Divination is defined as 'an attempt to discover the unknown through experts and their various devices.' The author describes a specific form of divination entitled 'Ngam,' which is widespread among the Kaka culture in the former British Cameroons. Ngam divination centres around a set of 'leaf-cards' with various imprinted symbols, the 'diviner,' and a spider. It is through the interpretation of the leaf-cards as manipulated by either the diviner or the spider that the unknown or supernatural can be understood. An examination is made of the Kaka culture and more precisely the social setting, variability, and social significance of Ngam divination.

57 **Les Gbaya.** (The Gbaya.)
John Hilberth. Uppsala, Sweden: Studia Ethnographica
Upsaliensia, 1962. 142p. (Studia Ethnographica Upsaliensia, XIX).

The first four chapters focus on the material, social, and family life of Gbaya, and on their mythology, religion, and magic. Chapter five examines various aspects of the Gbaya language, including conjugation of verbs, sentence structure, prepositions, and adjectives. The final two chapters are collections of Gbaya proverbs, legends, and tales. The text is complemented by numerous figures and a glossary of Gbaya words.

58 **La structure sociale des Bamiléké.** (The social structure of the Bamileke.)
J. Hurault. Paris: Mouton, 1962. 133p. 4 maps. (Le Monde d'Outre-mer Passé et Présent: Deuxième Série).

This is a study of the parentage system and social structure of the Bamileke people. A comparison is made of various 'chefferies' or chiefdoms within Bafoussam, which is a Bamileke subdivision. The author asserts that there are two basic types of customs present among sub-Saharan peoples. The first is the 'theoretical custom' which is discovered through interrogation. The second is the 'real custom,' which is not only different from the theoretical custom, but is also largely unknown to investigation. It is the purpose of this study to separate the 'real' from the 'theoretical.' The five major sub-divisions of the book discuss Bamileke material life, parentage system, and family customs and customary rights, as well as the functioning of the chiefdom and neighbourhoods. The appendixes provide an interesting portrayal of Bamileke beliefs and the future of Bamileke institutions. Several studies of Bamileke society were undertaken at this time as part of France's effort to undermine the left-wing Union des Populations du Cameroun, (UPC) which was quite active in the Bamileke region.

59 **Les bases de l'organisation sociale chez les Mouktélé (Nord-Cameroun): structures lignagées et mariage.** (The foundations of social organization among the Muktele (North Cameroon): lineage structures and marriage.)
Bernard Juillerat. Paris: Université de Paris, 1971. 271p. 10 maps. bibliog.

This is the first comprehensive ethnographic study of the Mouktele. The author utilizes two basic plans of action to study lineage and marriage structures. Firstly, a diachronic analysis is presented in order to determine the historical process by which patrilineages were created or destroyed and grouped together or dispersed. An examination is made of immigration and internal 'micro-migration' factors. Secondly, there is a synchronic analysis of segmentary organization *vis-à-vis* the functions and different types of Mouktele authority. Various subjects discussed in the study include interlineage relations, ritual functions and authority, lineage structures and armed conflict, the exogamous system and polygamy. The topic of marriage is comprehensively covered, and includes discussions of prematrimonial relations, matrimonial rites, and the breakdown of marriage.

60 **Women of the grassfields: a study of the economic position of women in Bamenda, British Cameroons.**
Phyllis M. Kaberry, preface by Daryll Forde. London: HM Stationery Office, 1952. 220p. 2 maps.

The central theme of this study is the role of women in the Bamenda economy. An examination is made of women's attitudes toward their occupation, rights to property, working conditions, and agricultural methods. These factors are examined in relation to the way they affect women's status and standing within kinship groups and within the community as a whole. The author concludes that any plans for economic development must take into account the women's role in society for it is she who assumes the major responsibility for subsistence crops. An extensive appendix provides several yearly budgets for individual Bamenda families.

61 **Witchcraft of the sun: incest in Nso.**
Phyllis M. Kaberry. In: *Man in Africa*. Edited by Mary Douglas, Phyllis M. Kaberry. Garden City, New York: Anchor Books, 1971, p. 177-97. bibliog.

Dr. Kaberry remains one of the most outstanding students of Bamenda ('Grasslands') ethnography. Much of her work concentrated on the Kingdom of Nso or Nsaw. In this brief essay she presents some description of Nso society, with the emphasis on the concept of incest in that society. Marriage is discussed in some detail. Comparisons are made with other African societies in terms of the definition of incest, and the author argues that kinship structure is an important factor in the definition of incest.

62 **Les principautés Kotoko: essai sur le caractère sacré de l'autorité.**
(The Kotoko principalities: an essay on the sacred character of authority.)
Annie M. D. Lebeuf. Paris: Editions du Centre National de la Recherche Scientifique, 1969. 388p. 4 maps. bibliog. (Etudes et Documents de l'Institut d'Ethnologie).

This volume is one of a series of publications which examine the ancient Chad civilization of Sao. The 'inheritor' of Sao and the subject of this study are the Kototo, a river people located on the Chari and Logone Rivers of Northern Cameroon. The author introduces the book by situating the Kototo in terms of geography, demography, and history. The first section examines the origins and constitution of the Kototo principalities. The second section describes the role of political authority; who embodies it, how it is exercised, and how it maintains cohesion among the various principalities. The final section analyses the 'sacredness' of authority in terms of various 'functions.' Included are the nomination and enthroning of the prince and dignitaries and emblems of power, etiquette, and religious ceremonies in terms of the role played by the prince. Also see this author's essay in C. Tandit's ed., *Contribution de la recherche ethnologique à l'histoire des civilisations du Cameroun*, vol. I. (Paris: CNRS, 1981.).

Peoples

63 **L'Habitation des Fali: montagnards du Cameroun septentrional.**
(The Fali home: highlanders of Northern Cameroon.)
Jean-Paul Lebeuf.   Paris: Librairie Hachette, 1961. 607p. 16 maps.
bibliog.

Lebeuf's account of the mountain-dwelling Fali people is one of a series of ethnographical studies aimed at the elucidation of the cultures and peoples of Northern Cameroon. The first section examines the history, geographical setting, habitat, material life, and religion of the Fali, while the second part explores the social aspect of living conditions. The author analyses the composition of the family and day-to-day living, and studies the way in which foreign influences have influenced basic living conditions. The final section examines Fali myths, explaining how household furnishings and utensils acquire their cosmological and anthropomorphical significations.

64 **Kirdi, les populations païennes du Nord-Cameroun.** (Kirdi, the
pagan populations of North Cameroon.)
Bertrand Lembezat.   Yaoundé: L'Institut Français d'Afrique
Noire, 1950. 101p. 3 maps. bibliog. (Série: Populations, no. 2).

This is an anthropological study of the Kirdi who inhabit Northern Cameroon. The common characteristics of the numerous Kirdi peoples are specified in terms of the social and material aspects of their lives and specific beliefs, myths, fables, and legends. The particular traits which differentiate the various groups are also discussed according to geographical zones of inhabitation (groups of the plain, groups of the mountains, and those that live in between).

65 **Mukulehe: un clan montagnard du Nord-Cameroun.** (Mukulehe: a
highland clan of North Cameroon.)
Bertrand Lembezat.   Paris: Berger-Levrault, 1952. 228p. map.
bibliog.

This account of the author's one year stay with the Mukulehe, a people numbering close to 2,000 individuals and nestled in the Mandara Mountains of North Cameroon, is unique in that it is written by a former administrator of 'la France d'outre-mer' who had the opportunity to live among the Mukulehe early in his career. The author presents his findings in a graceful fashion, almost as if he was telling a story to the reader. The book is divided into three sections. The first examines the material life of the Mukulehe, with the second discussing their social life. The author is especially intrigued by the 'funeral urns' and their role in Mukulehe life. The final section examines the role of the supernatural, stressing the importance given to dreams, sickness, sacred rocks, fables, and legends.

66 **Les populations païennes du Nord-Cameroun et de l'Adamaoua.**
(The pagan populations of North Cameroon and Adamawa.)
Bertrand Lembezat.   Paris: Presses Universitaires de France, 1961.
252p. map. bibliog. (Monographies Ethnologiques Africaines).

This is a comprehensive survey of the 'pagan' peoples or non-Muslim ethnic groups which inhabit Northern Cameroon. The first half of the book is an exploration of the mountain dwelling peoples of Mandara (Matakam, Mofu,

24

apsiki and Margui), the river peoples of Logone (Mousgoum, Massa and oupouri), and those groups situated between the mountains and the plains 3uisiga, Moundang, Guidar and Daba). Each group is examined in terms of its nguistics, physical environment, economic life, social organization, and key iltural traits. The second half of the book is devoted to the peoples of the enoue area (Fali, Namchi and Bata) and those situated in the Adamawa region Mboum, Bourou and Baboute).

7 **Progress in the past: dilemmas of wealth in Bakosi.**
Michael Levin. In: *Perceptions of development*. Edited by Sandra Walliman. London: Cambridge University Press, 1977, p. 78-86.

he purpose of the study is to examine the dilemmas and contradictions onfronted by members of Bakossi society who became wealthy by growing cocoa nd coffee. The Bakossi are described as becoming rich within their own lands by orking within 'traditional structures,' the transformation of which has created a nique dilemma; namely, 'How to maintain the solidarity of an increasingly ratified and occupationally mobile population?' The author argues that aditional aspects of Bakossi society and history provide the context for this dlemma, also constituting the Bakossi rationale for current attitudes to change nd the future.

8 **Le Matakam du Cameroun: essai sur le dynamique d'une société préindustrielle.** (The Matakam of Cameroon: an essay on the dynamic of a preindustrial society.)
Jean-Yves Martin. Paris: ORSTOM, 1970. 215p. 16 maps. bibliog.

n this ethnographic analysis of the Matakam peoples of Northern Cameroon the ithor argues that Matakam institutions (social, economic and political) are articular responses' to three specific variables: geographic, historic and emographic, which are seen as both resources and constraints. The underlying inction of Matakam institutional response is economic, social, and cultural urvival.' The first section of the study examines Matakam societal variables and llage life. A further analysis is made of the organization of subsistence farming, eproduction, and matrimonial alliances. A comparison is made between the llage community and the political and religious communities, with the onclusion discussing the interplay of ethnic groups and the nation.

9 **Histoire et coutumes des Bamum.** (History and customs of the Bamum.)
Sultan Njoya, translated from the Bamum by Pasteur Henri Martin. Yaoundé: l'Institut Français d'Afrique Noire, Centre du Cameroun, 1952. 271p. (Série: Populations no. 5).

he translation of this account of the history and customs of the Bamum people an important ethnographical contribution in that the original is written in a inguage that in 1952 was only known to a few dozen people in the world. The riginal was microfilmed, with the microfilm being deposited at the Musée de Homme in Paris and the original being returned to the Palace of Foumban. This ablication, which includes an appendix which adds to the general comprehension f the text, is based on the oral history of Bamum as collected under the direction f Sultan Njoya.

Peoples

70 **The core culture of Nso.**
Mzeka N. Paul, introduction by Dan N. Lantum. Kimbo Nso, Cameroon: the author, 1980. 121p. 4 maps. bibliog.
The author presents an examination of the socio-political and cultural dynamics which enabled the Nso civilization to maintain a complex system of government foreign relations with neighbouring kingdoms, and the promotion of internal social progress during and after the colonial experience. Based largely on oral accounts, the author examines Nso cultural solidarity in terms of cultural and functional relationships, the evolution and development of cults, and the role of the Fon and women within traditional Nso society.

71 **The Fon of Bafut.**
Pat Ritzenthaler. New York: Thomas Y. Crowell, 1966. 221p. 2 maps. bibliog.
An account of the life of a Fon or chief who leads his three hundred year old Bafut kingdom to independence in the 20th century. The author provides a rich analysis of the customs and ceremonies that surround the daily life of this 'boy become king' and the impact that he has on the traditional Bafut society. With a few exceptions, the characters presented are 'composite personalities' based on legend, historical fact, British government reports, and personal observations.

72 **Cameroons village: an ethnography of the Bafut.**
Robert Ritzenthaler, Pat Ritzenthaler. Milwaukee, Wisconsin: Milwaukee Public Museum, 1962. 147p. map. bibliog. (Milwaukee Public Museum Publications in Anthropology, no. 8).
The authors chose Bafut as the subject of an ethnographical study because it represented 'an operative African kingdom, a phenomenon becoming rare in Africa.' The result is a 'three-dimensional' (written word, sound, and sight) documentation of the Bafut kingdom, including such topics as the supernatural, love and learning, the life cycle, economic life, and the role of the Fon. The book is enhanced by over sixty photographs presented as representative of the various aspects of Bafut society. Further insights on Bafut society can be gained from the fictional accounts by Gerald Durrell.

73 **Leopards and leaders.**
Malcolm Ruel. London, New York: Tavistock Publications, 1969. 345p. 2 maps. bibliog.
This is a political anthropological study of a Cross River people, the Banyang. One level of analysis is aimed at describing the Banyang political structure in terms of community organization, the principles which define their members coallegiance, and the institutions which play a role in government. The study's primary concern, however, is to examine the political processes which complement the Banyang political structures. These processes are examined in two basic fashions. Firstly, an analysis is made of the way authoritative decisions are made within small residential communities. Secondly, the processes which influence the constituted organization of the communities are brought to light. The author adds that the book's structural and processual analysis is an attempt to describe these terms in close adherence to the Banyang's sense of the concepts and values which can be considered to be political.

26

74 **From Pagan to Pullo: ethnic identity change in Northern Cameroon.**
Emily A. Shultz. *Africa*, vol. 54, no. 1 (1984), p. 46-64.
This article centres on the nature of ethnic identity in Guider, a small town of
Northern Cameroon. More precisely, the process of change in ethnic identity, or
the incorporation of Pagan peoples into the Fulbe (singular Pullo) ethnic group is
explored.

75 **Appellations et attitudes: le système de parenté Vouté.** (Kin terms
and attitudes: the Vute kinship system.)
Jean-Louis Siran. *L'Homme*, vol. 21, no. 3 (July-Sept. 1981), p.
36-69.
Vute kinship terms and their relationship to apparent kin attitudes are analysed,
and the article also inlcudes a typology of marriage practices and kin designations.

76 **Traditions et transition: entretiens avec des femmes Beti du Sud-
Cameroun.** (Traditions and transition: interviews with Beti women
of South Cameroon.)
Jeanne-Françoise Vincent, preface by Denise Paulme. Paris:
ORSTOM and Editions Berger-Levrault, 1976. 166p. 2 maps.
bibliog.
This study is the result of interviews with Beti women that the author
implemented between 1967 and 1971. Short sections describe marriage and the
precolonial situation of women, ancient women's rites, magic and sorcery, as well
as women's reactions to Christianity. The majority of the book, however, is
devoted to the written reproduction of the author's interviews with fourteen Beti
women. An excellent index of various women's 'themes' discussed is included.

77 **Place et pouvoir de la femme dans les montagnes Mofu (Nord-
Cameroun).** (Place and power of the woman in the Mofu mountains
(Northern Cameroon).)
Jeanne-Françoise Vincent. *Cahiers d'Etudes Africaines*, vol. 19,
no. 1-4 (1979), p. 225-51.
The author describes the role and power of women in the Mofu mountains of
Northern Cameroon. Vincent presents a more general discussion of the Mofu in
her essay in *Contribution de la recherche ethnologique à l'histoire des civilisations
du Cameroun*, vol. I, edited by C. Tandits, (Paris: CNRS, 1981.).

African clearings.
See item no. 120.

Black sheep, adventures in West Africa.
See item no. 178.

An African trail.
See item no. 179.

Peoples

Aristocrats facing change: the Fulbe in Guinea, Nigeria, and Cameroon.
See item no. 231.

Village communities and the state: changing relations among the Maka of Southeastern Cameroon since the colonial conquest.
See item no. 263.

Limits to ritual resolution in Meta society.
See item no. 298.

Capital punishment in egalitarian society: the Meta' case.
See item no. 299.

Les institutions de droit public du pays Bamiléké (Cameroun): évolution et régime actuel. (The evolution of public law in Bamileke Country (Cameroon): evolution and current regime.)
See item no. 303.

Miscellany of Maroua Fulfulde (Northern Cameroon).
See item no. 439.

Fulfulde tales of Northern Cameroon II.
See item no. 440.

History

78 **The Lamibe of Fombina: a political history of Adamawa, 1809-1901.**
Sa'ad Abubakar, foreword by Iya Abubakar. Zaria, Nigeria;
Oxford, England: Ahmadu Bello University Press and Oxford
University Press, 1977. 190p. 2 maps. bibliog.
This pioneering work examines the role of the *jihad* in West African history.
More specifically, the author examines the *jihad* in Fombina and the subsequent
rise of the Emirate. With the advent of colonial rule, however, the Emirate
disappeared as a political entity, with its peoples being divided between Nigeria
and Cameroon. The author first introduces the region and its various peoples,
pointing out the significance of the Fulbe of Fombina and their *jihad*. An analysis
is made of the founding of the Emirate, and the processes of expansion,
consolidation, and conflict are specified. Finally, the volume analyses the decline
and collapse of the Emirate, followed by 20th-century developments in Fombina.

79 **Historical notes on the scheduled monuments of West Cameroon.**
Edwin W. Ardener. Buea, Cameroon: Ministry of Education and
Social Welfare and West Cameroon Antiquities Commission, 1965.
16p.
The purpose of this booklet is to inform both Cameroonians and foreign visitors
of the 'wealth of history' represented by the scheduled monuments of West
Cameroon. Detailed notes are provided on historic sites such as the Bismarck
Fountain in Buea, the fort at Bamenda, the Prime Minister's Lodge in Buea and
the Senior District Officer's House in Victoria. A list of unscheduled sites, several
of which are in the Western Grassfields, is also included. Photographs of the
scheduled monuments accompany the text.

History

80 **Eye-witnesses to the annexation of Cameroon, 1883-1887.**
Shirley G. Ardener. Buea, Cameroon: Ministry of Primary
Education and West Cameroon Antiquities Commission, 1968. 88p.
map. bibliog.
This booklet attempts to elucidate the events of Cameroon's annexation by
Germany between 1883 and 1887 by combining translated portions of eye-witness
accounts and historical hindsight. Extracts are taken from Thomas Lewis' *These
seventy years* and Carl Scholls' *Nach Kamerun!* A short introduction describes the
lives of Thomas Lewis and Carl Scholl and subsequent sections study the nature
of Victoria and Douala before annexation (with especial reference to the year
1883), the 1884 annexations, the Douala War, the final consolidation of the
protectorate and the subsequent British withdrawal. There are three appendixes
entitled: 'British treaties with West Cameroon peoples, from 1884;' 'British
treaties with East Cameroon peoples, from 1840;' and 'Woermann's instructions
to Schmidt, 1884.'

81 **Duala versus German in Cameroon: economic dimensions of a
political conflict.**
Ralph A. Austen. *Revue Française d'Histoire d'Outre-Mer*, vol.
64, no. 237 (1977), p. 477-97.
German colonial efforts to expropriate the urban landholdings of the Duala at the
beginning of the 20th century are discussed. A struggle ensued between the Duala
and the Germans which culminated in 1914 with the execution of the prominent
Duala chief, Manga Bell. The author argues that from an economic viewpoint the
struggle was not rational; 'the Germans did not need to expropriate and Duala
prosperity depended more upon rural plantations than urban land.' Furthermore,
German colonial actions ensured the evolution of the Duala into a kind of
'parasitic' élite in direct opposition to European economic motives.

82 **Slavery among coastal middlemen: the Duala of Cameroon.**
Ralph A. Austen. In: *Slavery in Africa.* Edited by Suzanne Miers,
Igor Kopytoff. Madison, Wisconsin: University of Wisconsin
Press, 1977, p. 305-33. map. bibliog.
The author asserts that although the Duala of Cameroon have been misleadingly
stereotyped as 'slave-trading middlemen,' various forms of slavery did play a
crucial role in their historical development. The position of slaves within Duala
society at the middle of the 19th century is described at length. The majority of
the article is devoted to a description and analysis of the processes which
contributed to stratification within the Duala society as well as its substantial
change from the 18th to the 20th century.

83 **The metamorphoses of middlemen: the Duala, Europeans and the
Cameroon hinterland, ca. 1800- ca. 1960.**
Ralph A. Austen. *International Journal of African Historical
Studies*, vol. 16, no. 1 (1983), p. 1-24. map.
The Duala of Cameroon are described as 'quintessential precolonial middlemen'
who managed to retain their role in later Cameroon history as opposed to other

30

comparable groups along the West African coast. 'Protocolonial situations allowed for the development of a great number of middleman roles but created difficulties in definining a "national" African order which would succeed and transcend them.' Firstly, there is a description of the precolonial situation of the Duala as marked by 'hegemony, balance and disorder.' Secondly, internal change experienced by the Duala and the transition to formal colonialism is discussed. Thirdly, the nature of colonialism and the middlemen are examined. Finally, the author studies the Duala role in fostering ethnic hegemony, regional integration, and Cameroon nationalism.

84 **Martin Samba: face à la pénétration Allemande au Cameroun.**
(Martin Samba: opposition to German penetration in Cameroon.)
Madeleine Mbono Samba Azan with the assistance of Bernard
Rouzet.   Paris: ABC; Dakar, Abidjan: Nouvelles Editions
Africaines, 1976. 109p. map. bibliog. (Grandes Figures Africaines).

Martin Samba, or Mebenga m'Ebono, was born in the South Eastern portion of Cameroon in 1875. He studied with the Germans and became an infantry officer in their colonial army. Eventually he revolted against the Germans and led military attacks against them. Whether this was done for his personal gain or whether he was a true nationalist leader is open to some debate. This volume takes the latter view. Samba was defeated and executed by the Germans on the eve of the First World War.

85 **Histoire de Garoua: cité Peule du XIX siècle.** (History of Garoua: Fulani city of the 19th century.)
Ahmadou Bassoro, Eldridge Mohammadou.   Garoua, Cameroon:
ONAREST, Institut des Sciences Humaines, 1977. 296p. 9 maps.
bibliog. (Traditions Historiques des Foulbé de l'Adamawa, no. 3).

This anthropological study is the third in a series devoted to the historical traditions of the Foulbe of Adamawa in Northern Cameroon during the 19th century. This volume is devoted to a study of the Foulbe peoples of Garoua. Written in both French and Foulfoude, this study in particular and the series in general marks an important contribution to the study of the oral history and traditions of the Foulbe peoples.

86 **African questions at the Paris Peace Conference.**
George Louis Beer, introduction by Louis Herbert Gray.   New
York: Macmillan, 1923; London: Dawsons of Pall Mall, 1968. 628p.
8 maps. bibliog.

This classic work depicts the salience of African issues at the Paris Peace Conference as seen through the eyes of George Louis Beer, 'Chief of the Colonial Division of the American Delegation to Negotiate Peace.' The essays contained in this volume not only elucidate the colonial problem in Africa, but also have direct application to colonial situations throughout the world. After discussing the rise and specific aspects of the German colonies in Africa, there is a detailed analysis of the problems of international cooperation and control of middle Africa. An emphasis is placed on the economic aspects of these problems. Finally, colonial questions dealing with tropical and North Africa, German South West Africa, and the Pacific islands are presented. Extensive appendixes document various agreements, conventions, draft mandates, and treaties which are important to gaining an understanding of this period of history.

87 **The native problem in Africa.**
Raymond Leslie Beull. Cambridge, Massachusetts: Bureau of International Research, Harvard University and Radcliffe College, 1928; London: Cass, 1965. Vol. 2, p. 270-413 map. bibliog.

The purpose of this volume is twofold. Firstly, the author illuminates the problems that have arisen because of the contact of traditional African societies with the industrialized civilization of the West. Secondly, an attempt is made to show how and to what degree these problems are being solved by the governments involved. One case study examines the specific condition of the two French mandated territories of Togoland and the Cameroons. The author provides an overview of the mandates' administration and the fate of German property and missions under French rule. Official colonial native policy is reviewed in terms of how it generally improved the quality of native life. Finally, the political situation in the territories is discussed. This general study, while providing a case study of Cameroon, also presents a broader framework within which to evaluate the Cameroon situation.

88 **La colonisation des plaines par les montagnards au nord du Cameroun (monts Mandara).** (The colonization of the plains by the highlanders in the north of Cameroon (Mandara mountains).)
Jean Boutrais. Paris: ORSTOM, 1973. 277p. 31 maps. bibliog. (Travaux et Documents de l'ORSTOM, no. 24).

In this study of the colonization of the plains of Northern Cameroon by the highlanders of the Mandara Mountains, a presentation is made of the descent of the highlanders in the context of Northern Cameroon. This is followed by a discussion of the role of government administration, both pre- and post-colonial, in constraining and forcing the descent of the highlanders. Finally, the differences between 'directed' and 'spontaneous' colonization of the plains by the highlanders are analysed, and the consequences of highlander migration and colonization are described.

89 **Karnu's message and the 'War of the Hoe Handle': interpreting a Central African resistance movement.**
Philip Burnham, Thomas Christensen. *Africa*, vol. 53, no. 4 (1983), p. 3-22.

The Gbaya peoples number close to 500,000 and inhabit East Central Cameroon and the western third of the Central African Republic. This article examines the historical aspects (geographical scope, multi-ethnic character, and local variations in interpretation of the events) of the anti-colonial Gbaya rebellion, or Karnu Rebellion, under the inspirational leadership of Karnu. The rebellion is known as the 'War of the Hoe Handle' in the Gbaya language.

0   The Cameroons.
Albert F. Calvert.   London: T. Werner Laurie, 1917. 82p. 9 maps.
There is some interesting descriptive material in this book, including more than
90 photographs, of the German colony of Cameroon. Colonial education,
agriculture and plantation development, and the border with the British colony of
Nigeria are major topics in this analysis of German colonial administration. Both
mission and administrative schools are examined under the subject of 'Native
ducation.'

1   The British and the Northern Kamerun problem 1919-1961.
Bongfen Chem-Langhee.   *Abbia*, nos. 38-40 (May 1982), p. 309-31.
Prior to the Fulbe invasions of the early 19th century in Northern Cameroon and
the arrival of the Europeans, four main groups of peoples competed for control
and domination of the region. These major groups included the aborigines, the
Korofa, the Batta, and the Mandara. This article examines British manipulation
of these competing ethnic groups for self-serving purposes between 1919 and
961.

2   The origin of the Southern Cameroons House of Chiefs.
Bongfen Chem-Langhee.   *International Journal of African
Historical Studies*, vol. 16, no. 4 (1983), p. 653-73.
This article delineates the various factors which coalesced to produce the
Southern Cameroons House of Chiefs, an institution which lasted from 1960 to
972. Factors discussed include the precolonial political and administrative
organization of the territory, subsequent German and British colonial administra-
ion, events in Nigeria, the desires of the Western-educated élite, and the
determination of the traditional rulers of the area.

3   Rulers of empire: the French colonial service in Africa.
William B. Cohen.   Stanford, California: Hoover Institution Press,
Stanford University, 1971. 279p. 2 maps. bibliog.
This is an analysis of the 'corps of Colonial Administrators' which served in sub-
Saharan black Africa and Madagascar. The administration of French colonial
erritory was highly decentralized, with the empire being divided among three
separate ministries (colonies, foreign affairs, and interior) and five different
colonial services. The author argues that, as colonial administration was highly
decentralized, great authority was given to the administrators in the individual
erritories. Therefore, a complete understanding of French colonial rule
necessitates a study of this overseas-based élite. An examination is made of the
class background, geographical origins, formal training, and ideological outlooks
of France's colonial administrators. Special emphasis is placed on the importance
of formal training in France's 'Ecole Colonial' and 'Ecole Nationale de la France
Outre-Mer'.

History

94   **African history.**
Philip D. Curtin, Steven Feierman, Leonard Thompson, Jan
Vansina.   Boston, Massachusetts: Little, Brown; London:
Longman, 1978. 612p. 55 maps.

A basic introduction to the history of the continent. Although there is not a
separate section on Cameroon, this work serves as an excellent background for
understanding Cameroon history.

95   **Health and disease on the plantations of Cameroon, 1884-1939.**
Mark W. DeLancey. In: *Disease in African history.* Edited by
Gerald W. Hartwig, K. David Patterson.   Durham, North
Carolina: Duke University Press, 1978, p. 153-79. 2 maps.

One of the most significant economic developments during the German colonial
period was the opening of numerous large, privately-owned plantations along the
coast and around Mt. Cameroon. Today these plantations are owned by the
Cameroon government as the Cameroon Development Corporation. Forced
labour was used in the plantations by the Germans and in the early years, there
were extremely high death rates among these workers. Changes in climate, food,
and living conditions were the major causes of the high mortality rate. Workers
were drawn from relatively cool, dry areas at high elevations inland, to work at
hot, damp, low elevations on the coast. A low level of medical care and a lack of
knowledge of tropical diseases contributed to the mortality rate.

96   **Sur les chemins du développement: essai d'histoire des faits
économiques du Cameroun.** (On the paths of development: essay on
the history of the economic events of Cameroon.)
F. Etoga Eily, preface by Charles Onana Awana.   Yaoundé:
Centre d'Edition et de Production de Manuels et d'Auxiliaires de
l'Enseignement, 1971. 521p. 7 maps. bibliog.

The author provides a comprehensive picture and analysis of the economic
aspects of Cameroon's development and how these have varied at different
periods in the nation's history. First, there is a presentation of Cameroon's society
and economic system before the arrival of the Europeans. Second, the rise and
subsequent demise of the West African slave trade along with the introduction of
European 'trusts' are examined in terms of their economic effects on Cameroon.
Third, a description is made of Germany's thirty years of occupation and its
specific form of colonial economic organization. Finally, the economic aspects of
Cameroon as a mandated territory under British and French tutelage are
portrayed. The author relies heavily on official French sources for the latter
portion of the book.

97   **A history of the Cameroon.**
Tambi Eyongetah, Robert Brain.   London: Longman, 1974. 192p.
12 maps. bibliog.

This general history of Cameroon emphasizes the region of West or anglophone
Cameroon. The authors argue that this region deserves a 'history of its own'
because of its 'separate character' and the fact that it forms a unique 'cultural

34

unit' within the Cameroon Republic. An analysis is made of language distribution, cultural innovations, ethnic movements, and political developments in order to illuminate the general patterns of Cameroon's historical development.

98   **The Prime Minister's Lodge, Buea.**
      Margaret Field.   Buea, Cameroon: Ministry of Primary Education and West Cameroon Antiquities Commission, 1969. 23p.

This booklet provides a detailed account of the Prime Minister's lodge in Buea. The first half describes the building of the lodge, its unique features and furniture, and the legends which are associated with it. The second half details the general qualities and special features of the lodge's gardens, including its notable plants and rose garden. An appendix provides a list of the occupants of the lodge who held significant positions. The building was constructed by the Germans to house their governor.

99   **The rulers of German Africa, 1884-1914.**
      L. H. Gann, Peter Duignan.   Stanford, California: Stanford University Press, 1977. 286p. 3 maps.

This is the first of a series of books which aims to analyse the social structure of the European colonial services in Africa. It studies the administrative perform-ance, ideology, and educational and class backgrounds of German colonial personnel who were assigned to the territories of German East Africa, South West Africa, Cameroon, and Togo. The author's main hypothesis is that even though Germany's holdings in Africa played a minor role in terms of overall German trade and foreign investment, the colonies were nonetheless extremely affected by German rule. The authors argue that there was in essence a 'double-edged' effect of colonial rule. While conquest involved a great deal of violence and brutality, the German administrative structure is seen as having many positive effects such as the building of a basic infrastructure, encouragement of new forms of economic enterprise, and the introduction of European technology.

100   **Cameroon: United Nations challenge to French policy.**
      David E. Gardinier, foreword by Philip Mason.   London, New York: Oxford University Press, 1963. 142p. map. bibliog.

Professor Gardinier is one of the earlier American students of Cameroon history, and he studied with the first of this group, Dr. Rudin. In this work, Gardinier traces the effects of United Nations' (UN) trusteeship on the relation between France and Cameroon, with emphasis on areas of conflict between France and the United Nations. Did trusteeship make any difference? Gardinier argues that it made a significant difference both in the timing and in the content of political development and independence in Cameroon. This is an important study based on field and archival research. It is one of the very few pieces of research on the effects of the role of the United Nations in colonial Africa.

101 **Douala: ville et histoire.** (Douala: town and history.)
René Gouellain.   Paris: Institut d'Ethnologie, Musée de
l'Homme, 1975. 402p. 18 maps. bibliog.

Relying heavily on archival material, the author attempts to clarify the historical evolution of the colonial city of Douala in terms of its genesis and main characteristics. A comparison is made between the pre-colonial and colonial periods and the influences they had on the general evolution of the city. An examination of the pre-colonial period explains the peopling of South Western Cameroon, the relationship between the diverse migrant groups, and their establishment in commercial trade. It is the Douala who occupied the primary position in this commercial trade. An examination of the colonial period shows the general subjugation of the Douala by the colonial power and the formation of an urban population composed of foreigners and indigenous natives. It is through colonial tutelage in the urban areas that trade unions and political parties were born in Douala, ultimately leading to independence.

102 **Cameroon.**
Great Britain. Historical Section, Foreign Office.   London: HM
Stationery Office, 1920. 83p. bibliog. (Handbook, no. 111).

This is a short and concise general handbook of Cameroon. The volume presents social, political, and economic conditions as they existed in the territory at the beginning of the 19th century. A chronological political history of Cameroon is also provided. Copies of the 1893 boundary agreement between Germany and Great Britain and the 1911 Franco-German Convention are included.

103 **Cameroun Togo.** (Cameroon Togo.)
Eugène Guernier, René Briat.   Paris: Le Haut Commissariat de la
République Française au Cameroun, 1951. 574p. (Encyclopédie de
l'Afrique Française).

This volume is one of a general series on French colonial territories published by the French colonial government. The encyclopaedia contains a wealth of knowledge encompassing the cultural, military, economic, and political realms. Especially useful are various sections which document French colonial expenses, import/export duties and payments, and other aspects of French colonial rule in both Cameroon and Togo. The Cameroon section of the volume occupies 390 pages.

104 **The food economy and French colonial rule in Central Cameroon.**
Jane I. Guyer.   *Journal of African History*, vol. 19, no. 4 (1978),
p. 577-97.

French administrative policies in Central Cameroon during the interwar period fostered the development of an indigenous class of chiefs. These chiefs mobilized manpower and resources within the rural areas to develop the European sector of the economy. Agricultural growth was therefore channeled through the chiefs rather than being left to market forces. The net result was the guaranteed flow of a cheap, reliable supply of food to the wage-earning population and the development of a wealthy class of planters who supported colonial administration. The impractibility of the system caused its abandonment in the 1930s in favour of a system based on family-based production units, although this system lacked an appropriate well-developed institutional framework.

105 **Female farming and the evolution of food production patterns amongst the Beti of South-Central Cameroon.**
Jane I. Guyer. *Africa*, vol. 50, no. 4 (1980), p. 341-56.
The central argument of this study is that the continuities and the changes in the evolution of Beti food production patterns 'are related to the way in which the Beti division of labour by sex has adjusted to the cash-cropping of cocoa.' Firstly, the Beti food economy is reconstructed as it functioned before the penetration of the colonial economy. Secondly, changes in the Beti food economy over a period of time are documented, employing published studies and data obtained from field research in two Eton villages.

106 **Head tax, social structure, and rural incomes in Cameroun: 1922-1937.**
Jane I. Guyer. Brookline, Massachusetts: Boston University, African Studies Center, [n.d.]. 37p. map. (Working paper, no. 3).
The author argues that Cameroon's rural population became a 'peasantry' during the interwar period. By focusing on the local impact of colonial taxation policy during this period, the article claims that 'the colonial mode of production, with high direct taxation and heavy reliance on obligatory measures, had a different impact on peasant incomes according to local conditions.' An understanding is necessary of the indigenous élites' interests and their changing relationship with the people and the colonial government in order to clarify the economic behaviour of particular local populations which became the peasantry. This study is also available in the journal *Cahiers d'Etudes Africaines* (vol. 20, no. 79 (1980), p. 305-29.)

107 **The culture policy of the Basel Mission in the Cameroons, 1886-1905.**
Erik Halldén. Lund, Sweden: University of Uppsala, 1968. 142p. map. bibliog. (Studia Ethnographica Upsaliensia, no. 31).
The primary purpose of this study is to 'present the culture factors affecting the Basel Mission and its attitudes in relation to the German colonial policy in the Cameroons.' The primary source material employed is the unprinted documents preserved in the archives of the Basel Mission. The author first discusses some problems in the 'history of ideas' which are pertinent to the Basel Mission. He goes on to study the emergence of the German Reich as a colonial power and its historical significance for the Basel Mission between 1884 and 1886. The Basel Mission as a factor in colonial and cultural policy in the Cameroons from 1887 to 1895 is examined; and finally, the relationship between the Basel Mission and plantation policy in the Cameroons from 1895 to 1905 is considered.

108   **Deutsche Kolonialherrschaft in Afrika: Wirtschaftsinteressen und Kolonial Verwaltung in Kamerun vor 1914.** (German colonial rule in Africa: economic interests and colonial administration in Cameroon before 1914.)
Karin Hausen.   Freiburg, GFR: Atlantis Verlag, 1970. 340p.
2 maps. bibliog.

German economic interests and colonial administration in Cameroon before 1914 are the major topics of this study. The author discusses Germany's colonial policy in terms of German domestic political interest groups, the structure of the colonial bureaucracy, and the effects that it had on traditional Cameroon societal and cultural patterns. Special emphasis is placed on the role of German interest groups in Cameroon. An analysis is made of how conflicts between interest groups as well as with the colonial government ultimately affected Germany's colonial policies in Cameroon.

109   **Radical nationalism in Cameroun: social origins of the UPC rebellion.**
Richard A. Joseph.   Oxford, England: Oxford University Press, 1977. 383p. 5 maps. bibliog.

Basing his conclusions on data gathered from extensive interviews and analysis of archival and published materials, Richard Joseph overturns many of the earlier ideas about the Union des Populations du Cameroun (UPC), the Cameroon independence movement, and the role of white settlers in Cameroon. This study is a thorough historical analysis of the highest quality. Joseph argues that the UPC was the first real nationalist party in francophone Cameroon, but that its goals of true independence from France and socialist development in Cameroon were more than the French colonial administration, settlers, and commercial interests were willing to accept. The French forced the UPC into exile and rebellion, thereby preventing them from taking part in the electoral process and allowing the French to use police and military force to destroy the UPC. While this went on, the French could develop other, more amenable, Cameroon leadership to take over at independence. A French-language edition will soon be published.

110   **Church, state, and society in colonial Cameroun.**
Richard A. Joseph.   *International Journal of African Historical Studies*, vol. 13, no. 1 (1980), p. 5-32.

The author first describes missionary intervention along the Cameroons coast in the precolonial period and the special problems which were caused by the successive involvement of British, German, and French colonial forces. An emphasis is placed upon the role of the missionaries as intermediaries between the colonial authorities and the colonized peoples. It is shown how differing perceptions of what education and language were to yield in Cameroon could never be reconciled among three groups: the state wished to promote basic literacy and numeracy, the church desired indoctrination and practical training, and the Africans themselves wished to the prepared for remunerative careers.

11   **Political evolution in the Cameroons.**
      P. M. Kale.   Buea, Cameroon: the author, 1967. 93p.

P. M. Kale was one of the early political leaders in anglophone Cameroon. In this brief publication he portrays some aspects of his role in anglophone politics as well as describing some important features of Cameroon political history. Kale was resident in Nigeria at the time of the founding of the Cameroon Youth League, which was the first anglophone Cameroon nationalist organization. Kale was a founding member. In subsequent years he was prominent in various political organizatons and attended constitutional conferences in London. This work is an important record of the independence and reunification movements in the British Trust Territory and it provides valuable insights on the relationship between Nigeria and British Cameroons. Kale also wrote the useful, but very difficult to locate, *Brief history of the Bakweri*.

112   **Adamawa, past and present: an historical approach to the**
       development of a Northern Cameroons province.
       A. H. M. Kirk-Greene, foreword by Daryll Forde.   London, New
       York; Toronto: Oxford University Press for the International
       African Institute, 1958. 230p. 5 maps. bibliog.

The author, previously an officer in the British colonial administration of Nigeria, traces over 150 years of the history of the province of Adamawa. The sources employed include the vast number of narratives and records of travellers to Adamawa, as well as local reports, district notebooks, legends, and eyewitness accounts. A chronological record is presented which describes the early exploration of Adamawa, the creation of the Royal Niger Company, subsequent British occupation and administration, and the effects of the First World War. The rest of the book is devoted to a study of the development of general administration that occurred within the territory. Interesting appendixes denote the history of 'Provincial' headquarters, notes on the Fulani language, the Farer festival of Numan Division, initiation ceremonies, and judicial oaths in Adamawa. This part of British Cameroons eventually joined Nigeria.

113   **An economic history of tropical Africa.**
       Edited by Z. A. Konczacki, J. M. Konczacki.   London: Cass,
       1977. 3 vols. maps. bibliog.

Only the first two volumes, on precolonial and colonial Africa, are relevant to Cameroon. The third volume is devoted to Southern Africa.

114   **Yaoundé d'après Zenker (1895).** (Yaounde according to Zenker
       (1895).)
       Philippe Laburthe-Tolra.   Yaoundé: Faculté des Lettres et
       Sciences Humaines de Yaoundé, 1970. 113p. map. bibliog.

This French translation of Zenker's original work (in German) provides a valuable description of Yaoundé and its inhabitants at the time of the German occupation (1895). Zenker, a German colonial administrator, was present during the establishment of the German post at Yaoundé. Drawings and photographs and the original German text are included.

History

115 **Export crops and peasantization: the Bakosi of Cameroon.**
Michael D. Levin. In: *Peasants in Africa*. Edited by Martin
Klein. Beverly Hills, California: Sage, 1980, p. 221-41.

The author examines in detail the interplay between the production of export
crops and the peasantization of the rural dwellers, using the Bakossi of Cameroon
as a case study. The essay is based on field research.

116 **Historical dictionary of Cameroon.**
Victor T. LeVine, Roger P. Nye. Metuchen, New Jersey:
Scarecrow Press, 1974. 198p. map. bibliog. (African Historical
Dictionaries, no. 1).

This important and useful reference is in danger of becoming out of date. In
addition to the dictionary, the volume contains a list of abbreviations and
acronyms, a bibliographic essay as an 'Introduction to the Study of Cameroon,' a
chronology of Cameroon history, and an extensive bibliography.

117 **Douala Manga Bell: héros de la résistance Douala.** (Douala Manga
Bell: hero of the Douala Resistance.)
Iyé Kala Lobé. Paris: ABC, 1977. 110p. bibliog. (Grandes
Figures Africaines).

This biography of one of the heroes of Cameroon resistance against German
colonialism is written for the secondary school student and the general reader.
Douala Manga Bell was a traditional leader of the Douala people, the original
inhabitants of the area which is now the city of Douala. Just prior to the First
World War the German rulers of Cameroon attempted to drive the Douala
people from their lands for a variety of racial and economic reasons. Bell led the
resistance to this policy and, in the hysteria preceeding the war, was convicted of
treason and hung.

118 **The African mandates in world politics.**
Rayford W. Logan. Washington, DC: Public Affairs Press, 1948.
220p. map.

In this detailed study of the 'vicissitudes of the diplomatic negotiations and the
ramifications of public discussions' concerning Germany's lost colonial territories
in Africa, the author argues that the return of these colonies was a salient feature
of Germany's demands prior to the Second World War. A description of the
division of Germany's African empire among various colonial powers after the
First World War is followed by an analysis of rising German demands for their
return under the Weimar Republic and Hitler. Hitler is said to have called for a
'new Monroe Doctrine for Africa' or an agreement between Stalin and himself for
the sharing of the continent under the auspices of a 'New World Order.'

119 **Great Britain and Germany's lost colonies, 1914-1919.**
William Roger Louis. Oxford, England: Clarendon Press, 1967.
165p. 2 maps.

The author argues that Great Britain, in a quandary at the Paris Peace
Conference in 1919 as to how to effectively deal with 'the German problem,'

deliberately followed a policy of stripping Germany of its overseas possessions including Cameroon. The purpose of this policy was the achievement of security for the British empire, 'a goal . . . that could not be attained without the elimination of the German colonies.' Firstly, an analysis is made of imperial rivalries in the period directly preceding the First World War (1884-1914). This is followed by an examination of the war itself in terms of Allied conquest and annexation of the former German colonies. Finally, the mandates system, established in 1919, is discussed.

120 African clearings.
Jean Kenyon Mackenzie. Boston; New York: Houghton Mifflin, 1924. 270p.

This group of essays present the author's impressions of Cameroon, and they are the result of several years of living within the area. In flowing prose, the author paints a picture of Cameroon society in the 1920s. Titles which set the tone of the book include 'The unforgotten journeys,' 'Minor memories,' 'Of luxuries and hardships,' and 'Appreciations.' Several of the essays, such as 'The host,' 'The teacher,' 'The forest children,' and 'The blacksmith,' present character sketches of individuals who were characteristic of the times. One of the articles, 'Exile and postman,' was published in *Atlantic Classics* by the Atlantic Monthly Press. Kribi, Elat, and Ebolowa are the locations of most of the author's experiences.

121 Contribution à l'étude de la préhistoire au Cameroun septentrional.
(A contribution to the study of prehistory in Northern Cameroon.) Alain Marliac. Paris: ORSTOM, 1975. 104p. maps.

The author, a noted scholar of Cameroon history, provides a comprehensive overview of the prehistory of Northern Cameroon. Also see this author's essay 'L'état des connaissances sur le paléolithique et le néolithique du Cameroun' in *Contribution de la recherche ethnologique à l'histoire des civilisations du Cameroun*, edited by C. Tandits (Paris: CNRS, 1981.).

122 L'Age du fer au Cameroun septentrional: données chronologiques nouvelles sur le Diamaré. (The Iron Age in Northern Cameroon: new chronological facts about the Diamare.)
Alain Marliac. *Journal des Africanistes*, vol. 52, no. 1-2 (1982), p. 59-67.

New radiocarbon tests of four Northern Cameroon areas (Salak, Goray, Biou, and Bidzar) place the Iron Age of the area between the 5th and 11th centuries AD. Other datings from upper levels (said to be contaminated) would set Cameroon's Iron Age's chronological limit in the 17th or 18th centuries, AD.

123 Military operations: Togoland and the Cameroons, 1914-1916.
F. J. Moberly. London: HM Stationery Office, 1931. 469p. 14 maps. bibliog.

This is an extremely detailed history of British military operations in Togoland and the Cameroons during the First World War. Representing the official British account, the volume outlines various military campaigns, such as the British occupation of the Northern Railway and destruction of Chang, the first and unsuccessful advance on Yaoundé, and the final capture of Yaoundé from German occupation forces. Also included are sections which deal with Franco-Belgian progress in the South East of the Cameroons. The text is complemented by several appendixes which outline 'Terms of surrender,' ships and vessels utilized in the various campaigns, and a list of troops operating in the Cameroon as of January 1, 1916.

124 **L'Histoire de Tibati: chefferie Foulbe du Cameroun.** (The history of Tibati: Fulani chiefdom of Cameroon.)
Eldridge Mohammadou.   Yaoundé: Editions Abbia, 1965. 72p. 2 maps.

Tibati is located in Northern Cameroon. This small work portrays Tibati history from the advance of the Foulbe in Northern Cameroon to the arrival of the German colonial power. The author presents in chronological fashion the rise of Tibati rulers, conquests and rivalries, and the problem of succession. The study is based on oral history sources.

125 **L'Histoire des Peuls Ferobe du Diamare, Maroua et Pette.** (History of the Ferobe Fulani of Diamare, Maroua, and Pette.)
Edited by Eldridge Mohammadou.   Tokyo: Institute for the Study of Languages and Cultures of Asia and Africa, 1976. 409p. 10 maps. bibliog.

This volume presents the history of the Peuls Ferobe of Diamare, peoples of Northern Cameroon. The first and second sections are devoted to the specific histories of the Maroua and Pette peoples, and the text is written in Foulfoude as well as in French. Extensive footnotes clarify and complement both texts. Included are chronologically organized geneaological tables and numerous maps.

126 **Fulbe Hooseere: les royaumes Foulbe du plateau de l'Adamaoua au XIX siècle: Tibati, Tignère, Banyo, Ngaoundéré.** (Fulbe Hooseere: Fulani kingdoms of the Adamawa plateau in the 19th century: Tibati, Tignere, Banyo, Ngaoundere.)
Eldridge Mohammadou.   Tokyo: Institute for the Study of Languages and Cultures of Asia and Africa (ILCAA), 1978. 440p. 12 maps. (ILCAA African Languages and Ethnography, VIII).

This anthropological study is the fourth in a series devoted to the historical traditions of the Foulbe of Adamawa in Northern Cameroon during the 19th century. The first three volumes presented the Foulbe peoples of Maroua, Rey-Bouba, and Garoua; this volume is devoted to a study of the Foulbe peoples of Tibati, Tignere, Banyo and Ngaoundere. Written in both French and Foulfoude which is the language of the region, this volume in particular and the series in general makes an important contribution to the study of the oral history and traditions of the Foulbe peoples. Also see this author's essay in C. Tandits, ed. *Contribution de la research ethnologique à l'historie des civilisations du Cameroun.* vol. I (Paris: CNRS, 1981.).

127 **Ray ou Rey Bouba: traditions historiques des Foulbé de l'Adamawa.** (Ray or Rey Bouba: historical traditions of the Fulani of Adamawa.)
Eldridge Mohammadou, Alhaji Hamadjoda Abdoullaye.
Garoua, Cameroon: Musée Dynamique du Nord-Cameroun, ONAREST; Paris: Editions du Centre National de la Recherche Scientifique, 1979. 348p. 22 maps. bibliog.
This collection of the historical traditions of the Foulbe of Adamawa, describes the evolution of the *lamidat* of Ray ou Rey Bouba, an area situated in North Eastern Cameroon. The origins and migrations of the Foulbe into the region and the succession of various leaders throughout the *lamidat*'s existence form the basis of the study, which is written in both French and Foulfoulde. The text is complemented by extensive notes, annexes, chronological and genealogical tables, and detailed maps. An earlier, typescript version appeared in 1972.

128 **Histoire du Cameroun.** (Cameroon history.)
Engelbert Mveng. Paris: Présence Africaine, 1963. 533p. 21 maps. bibliog.
This is an extremely detailed and well documented history of Cameroon. The major historical periods discussed are the pre-historic age (before 500 AD), the Middle Ages (500-1500), the pre-colonial period (1500-1850 and 1850-1880), colonialism (1880-1919), mandated territory (1919-1945), trusteeship (1945-1960), and reunification. Each section contains documents relevant to the period. An extensive bibliography is classified by subject matter. This work is now available in a two-volume set, reprinted by the Centre d'Edition et de Production pour l'Enseignement et la Recherche in Yaoundé (1984).

129 **Manuel d'histoire du Cameroun.** (Manual of Cameroon history.)
Engelbert Mveng, D. Beling-Nkoumba. Yaoundé: Centre d'Edition et de Production pour l'Enseignement et la Recherche, 1978. 284p. 28 maps.
A standard history text designed for primary school students as well as those entering secondary education. The text is divided into fifty lessons which trace Cameroon history from prehistoric times to the present. The lessons are grouped under eight major subdivisions, with each representing a major historical period such as 'The colonial period (1880-1914).' Each lesson is followed by a short summary and study questions.

130 **Histoire des forces religieuses au Cameroon: de la première guerre mondiale à l'indépendence (1916-1955).** (History of religious forces in Cameroon: from the First World War to independence (1916-1955).)
Louis Ngongo. Paris: Editions Karthala, 1982. 298p. bibliog. (Hommes et Sociétés).
The author discusses the relationships between religion and politics.

43

131 **Fulani hegemony in Yola (old Adamawa), 1809-1902.**
M. Z. Njeuma. Yaoundé: the author, 1978. 298p. 7 maps.
The author discusses the origins, development, and principal characteristics of Fulani hegemony in Yola during the 19th century. The purpose of the study is to examine the actions of Fulani rulers within an overall political framework. More specifically, the author analyses how the Fulani rulers were responsible for founding the Emirate and for taking most of the political initiative that was needed to maintain it. The volume, which is divided into three main sections discusses the Fulani rise to power, the establishment of a central administrative core unit, and the arrival of the Europeans and subsequent invasion. The book is a shortened version of the author's PhD thesis.

132 **Njoya: réformateur du royaume Bamoun.** (Njoya: reformer of the Bamoun kingdom.)
Adamou Ndam Njoya. Paris: ABC; Dakar, Abidjan: Nouvelles Editions Africaines. 1977. [not paginated] map. (Grandes Figures Africaines).
King Njoya lived from 1867 to 1933 and ruled the Bamoun kingdom for much of this period. He came to power in 1885 and was forced into exile by the French in 1931. In this volume he is credited with resistance to the German occupation of his land, not by force but by studying the techniques that gave the Germans success and adapting these to the needs of the Bamoun people. Njoya was a scholar, an inventor, and a progressive ruler. He is well-known for the script he devised for the Bamoun language. The author of this volume is a scholar and political figure in Cameroon. Other interesting volumes in this series include *Martin Samba: face à la pénétration Allemande au Cameroun* (q.v.), and *Douala Manga Bell: héros de la résistance Douala.* (q.v.).

133 **Elements for a history of the western grassfields.**
Paul Nchoji Nkwi, Jean-Pierre Warnier. Yaoundé: University of Yaoundé, 1982. 236p. 9 maps. bibliog.
Nkwi, a Cameroonian trained in Switzerland, and Warnier, a Frenchman trained in the United States, are two of the most significant students of the history and anthropology of the Bamenda highlands or Grassfield area. Both have conducted sustained research in the area. In this volume they first discuss the general characteristics of the Western Grassfield chiefdoms and then examine specific examples from six regions of the Grassfield. The effort concentrates on the pre 1900 period but does attempt to analyse the fate of pre-colonial institutions for the post-1900 years. The volume is planned as a textbook and study-guide Questions are provided for each chapter.

134 **Traditional diplomacy, trade and warfare in the nineteenth century Western Grassfields.**
Paul Nchoji Nkwi. *Revue Science et Technique: Science and Technology Review* (Yaoundé), vol. 1, no. 3-4 (1983), p. 101-16, 3 maps. bibliog.
The dynamics of 19th-century Western Grassfields were complex and intricate

Despite hostile relations between the various political entities, there were significant diplomatic exchanges and trade. Nkwi reconstructs the history of these interactions from both oral and written sources.

135 **Great Britain and the final partition of the Cameroons: 1916-1922.**
Jide Osuntokun. *Afrika Zamani* (Yaoundé), vol. 6-7 (Dec. 1977), p. 53-71.

Cameroon was divided between Great Britain and France through a 'provisional' partition accord signed on March 16, 1916. The author argues that although both countries stressed the provisional nature of the agreement, local observers knew that France viewed the division of Cameroon as irrevocable and British officials considered the Cameroons as 'expendable in the overall interest of Great Britain's worldwide – strategy and territorial aspirations.' The article elucidates Great Britain's role in the partition of Cameroon and the succession of events between 1916 and 1922 in terms of its regional and international security interests.

136 **Beti society in the nineteenth century.**
Frederick Quinn. *Africa*, vol. 50, no. 3 (1980), p. 293-304.

The author reconstructs various aspects of traditional Beti society in the 19th century through the use of French and German archival material in Cameroon, German explorers' accounts, and oral interviews with Beti elders. Points discussed include Beti large groupings, warfare and feuding, regulating disputes, dancing the Bilabi, and an initiation rite.

137 **Charles Atangana of Yaoundé.**
Frederick Quinn. *Journal of African History*, vol. 21, no. 4 (1980), p. 485-95.

The author sketches the rise to prominence and power of Charles Atangana of Yaoundé (ca. 1880-1943), a Beti herdsman's son of Central Cameroon's rain forest. Relying neither on privileged birth nor military skills, Atangana at the age of 35 was chief of a group numbering nearly 500,000 people. Emphasis is placed on Atangana's dealings with first the German and then the French colonial powers.

138 **Germans in the Cameroons 1884-1914: a case study in modern imperialism.**
Harry R. Rudin. New Haven, Connecticut: Yale University Press, 1938. 456p. bibliog.

The purpose of this book is 'to give readers as complete a picture as possible of the operation of imperialism in the modern world.' The author analyses imperialism in the Cameroons in terms of the imperial administration in Germany and in the colony, emphasizing the 'dynamic elements' operating within this system. A summary is made of the German occupation and administration of the Cameroons, centering on the concept of 'home control.' The exploitation of the Cameroons is verified through trade and tariff figures, as well as by the examination of specific export products, such as rubber, coffee, and minerals. A further indication supporting the imperialism hypothesis is shown by an analysis of the deteriorating living and welfare conditions of the indigenous people. This standard work is the best available study in English of the German period.

45

139 **The history of Cameroon: once upon a time . . . Ahidjo.**
Serge Saint-Michel. Paris: Afrique Biblio Club, 1980. 48p. 3
maps.
This history of Cameroon is unique in that it is presented in comic book form
utilizing colour cartoons. Salient aspects of Cameroon's history, such as
colonialism, independence and reunification, are included, with the primary
emphasis on the rise of President Ahmadou Adidjo and his role in guiding the
destiny of the nation.

140 **Emergence et dissolution des principautés guerrières Vouté
(Cameroun Central).** (Emergence and dissolution of the Vute
warrior principalities (Central Cameroon).)
Jean-Louis Siran. *Journal des Africanistes*, vol. 50, no. 1 (1980),
p. 25-58.
The article traces the rise of the Vute warrior principalities in Cameroon as they
were pushed southward from Adamawa by Fulani conquests. The Vute were
forced to live like refugees until a subsequent generation of men trained in the art
of hunting destroyed the Vute unilineal (matrilineal) organization, killed the
former chief, and organized powerful slave hunting armies. The net result was a
series of Vute principalities completely dependent on the practice of war. This
state system collapsed with the imposition of a German colonial peace.

141 **Kamerun unter deutscher Kolonialherrschaft.** (Cameroon under
German colonial rule.)
Edited by Helmuth Stoecker. Vol. 1, Berlin: Rutten and
Loening, 1960. 288p. map. Vol. 2, Berlin: Veb Deutscher Verlag
der Wissenschaften, 1968. 272p. map.
This two volume set is a collection of essays which present various aspects and
topics of German colonial rule in Cameroon. The first volume contains four
articles which describe Germany's annexation of Cameroon, the insurrection of
the German-created native police in 1893, the rise and condition of the
Cameroonian worker class from 1895 to 1905, and the Cameroonian proletariat
between 1906 and 1914. The second volume also contains four articles. These
describe the German conquest and the native resistance struggles in the Southern
Cameroons (1884-1907), Germany's conquest of the North East, the creation of
'land concession societies,' and the historical origins of African anti-colonialism.
These essays are based on materials now contained in East German archives and
they represent a major contribution to the study of the history of the German
period. Volume 1 contains the following essays: 'Die deutsche Annexation', by
Hans-Peter Jaeck; 'Der Aufstand der Polizeisoldaten,' and 'Die Entstehung und
Lage der Arbeiterklasse unter dem deutschen Kolonialregime in Kamerun (1895-
1905)', by Adolf Ruger; and 'Das Kameruner Proletariat 1906-1914,' by Hella
Winkler. Volume 2 consists of essays by: Rudi Kaeselitz: 'Kolonialeroberung
und Widerstandskampf in Südkamerun (1884-1907)'; Helmuth Stoecker, Hartmut
Mehls, and Ellen Mehls: 'Die Eroberung des Nordostens'; Johanda Ballhaus:
'Die Landkonzessionsgesellschaften'; and, Adolf Ruger: 'Die Duala und die
Kolonialmacht, 1884-1914.'

142 **French Equatorial Africa and Cameroons.**
United Kingdom. Naval Intelligence Division. London: HM
Stationery Office, 1942. 524p. 100 maps. (Geographical Handbook
Series, no. BR 515).
This official British handbook of French Equatorial Africa was designed to
provide information for commanding officers of this time on countries that they
might be called upon to visit. Topics with direct naval significance include
descriptions of the coast and immediate hinterland, ports, communications, and
the administration of Equatorial Africa. Various sections also describe the
geological formations, climate, flora and fauna, diseases, and general distribution
of population in the area. Especially significant are the sections which deal with
agriculture, trade, mining, industry, and finance. This is an important reference
on conditions in French Cameroon in 1940.

143 **Histoire du peuplement et genèse des paysages dans l'ouest
Camerounais.** (History of the population and genesis of the
countrysides in West Cameroon.)
Jean-Pierre Warnier. *Journal of African History*, vol. 25, no. 4
(1984), p. 395-410.
It is argued that the exceptional linguistic diversity and density of West
Cameroon's Grassfields, the most recent archaeological discoveries there,
together with the ethnography of the region suggest that this area of Africa has
supported a continuously dense population for several millennia. Slash and burn
agriculture, the regional specialization of production, and the vicissitudes of the
historical peopling of the region are said to have contribiuted to the area's
linguistic diversity.

144 **Le Cameroun: les indigènes, les colons, les missions,
l'administration Française.** (Cameroon: natives, settlers, missions,
French administration.)
J. Wilbois. Paris: Payot, 1934. 256p. map.
The first half of this book describes the lives of the Cameroonians before the
arrival of the European colonialists. Included in the description are the family,
material, and religious aspects of day-to-day living. The second half of the book
presents the achievements of the colonial settlers, missionaries, and administrators.

L'Encyclopédie de la République Unie du Cameroun. (Encyclopaedia of
the United Republic of Cameroon.)
See item no. 3.

**Traditional Bamenda: the pre-colonial history and ethnography of the
Bamenda grassfields.**
See item no. 46.

Histoire et coutumes des Bamum. (History and customs of the Bamum.)
See item no. 69.

History

West African Pidgin-English: an historical overview.
See item no. 161.

One hundred years.
See item no. 166.

Origine et développement d'une église indépendente Africaine: l'église Baptiste Camerounaise. (Origin and development of an independent African church: the Cameroon Baptist church.)
See item no. 167.

The history of the Presbyterian church in West Cameroon.
See item no. 174.

The discipling of West Cameroon: a study of Baptist growth.
See item no. 175.

The Catholic church in Kom: its foundation and growth, 1913-1977.
See item no. 180.

Histoire de l'église en Afrique (Cameroun). (History of the church in Africa (Cameroon).)
See item no. 184.

Les origines de l'église évangélique du Cameroun: missions Européennes et Christianisme autochtone. (Origins of the evangelical church in Cameroon: European missions and native Christianity.)
See item no. 185.

Douala: un siècle en images. (Douala: a century in pictures.)
See item no. 222.

Ahmadou Ahidjo pionnier de l'Afrique moderne. (Ahmadu Ahidjo: pioneer of modern Africa.)
See item no. 232.

Territoires Africains sous mandat de la France: Cameroun et Togo. (African territories under French mandate: Cameroon and Togo.)
See item no. 251.

The Cameroons from mandate to independence.
See item no. 272.

The Cameroon Federal Republic.
See item no. 273.

Cameroon grassfield chiefs and modern politics.
See item no. 280.

Cameroun: an African federation.
See item no. 286.

Family and farm in Southern Cameroon.
See item no. 371.

Education in anglophone Cameroon, 1915-1975.
See item no. 394.

St. Joseph's College Sasse-Buea: a brief history (1939-1981).
See item no. 401.

Fulfulde tales of North Cameroon II.
See item no. 440.

German Africa: a select annotated bibliography.
See item no. 480.

German foreign policy, 1890-1914, and colonial policy to 1914: a handbook and annotated bibliography.
See item no. 482.

Languages

145 **Système verbal et prédicatif du Bulu.** (Verbal and predicative
system of the Bulu.)
Pierre Alexander. Paris: Klincksieck, 1966. 217p. bibliog.
(Langues et Littératures de l'Afrique Noire, no. 1).
The Bulu population is located in Southeastern Cameroon, and speaks a Bantu
language.

146 **Le problème linguistique au Cameroun.** (The Cameroon
linguistic problem.)
Henri Marcel Bot ba Njock. *Afrique et Asie*, no. 73 (1963), p. 3-
13.
The article summarizes and examines the language problem of Cameroon, a
nation with two official languages (French and English) which are foreign in
nature and numerous indigenous vernaculars. Rejecting the creation of a unique
national 'esperanto Camerounais' (Cameroon language), the author favours the
retaining of French and English as national languages, with indigenous languages
being supported and taught at the regional level. The teaching and promotion of
regional languages is deemed necessary if Cameroonians are to remain integrated
with their community of origin and their rich cultural heritage.

147 **Language and society in West Africa.**
C. M. B. Brann. *West African Journal of Modern Languages*,
vol. 3 (1978), p. 194-219.
Language questions are significant in Cameroon politics, law, education policy
and in many other aspects of life. Sociolinguistics, lingua franca, and language
policy are among the subjects included in this bibliography.

148 **More than 230 languages in Cameroon.**
Roland Breton, Michel Dieu. *Courier*, no. 80 (July-Aug. 1980), p. 92-95. map.

The authors assess Cameroon's attempt at forming an inventory and classifying into linguistic groups, sub-families, families, and phylums the languages and dialects spoken in Cameroon through the ALCAM system (Linguistic Atlas of Cameroon). An outline of the various languages extant in Cameroon is shown to confirm the 'singular diversity' and 'exceptional fragmentation' of Cameroon's linguistic situation.

149 **Cameroon home languages.**
Emmanuel Chia. In: *A sociolinguistic profile of urban centers in Cameroon.* Edited by Edna L. Koenig, Emmanuel Chia, John Povey. Los Angeles: Crossroads Press, 1983, p. 19-32. bibliog.

Professor Chia, of the University of Yaoundé, presents a new classification system for the almost 300 languages of Cameroon, excluding those spoken in Cameroon which are not native to the country. The classification of northern languages is considered in 'Les langues', by D. Barreteau, R. Breton and M. Dieu in *Le nord du Cameroun: des hommes, une région*, (Paris: ORSTOM, 1984), p. 159-80.

150 **L'Ecriture des Bamum.** (Writing of the Bamum.)
Idelette Dugast, M. D. W. Jeffreys. Douala, Cameroon: IFAN, 1950. 109p. map. bibliog. (Populations, no. 4).

The authors discuss the various alphabets invented by Sultan Njoya of Bamum, and also examine Bamum history and culture.

151 **An introduction to West African Pidgin English.**
David Dwyer, David Smith. East Lansing, Michigan: African Studies Center, Michigan State University for the US Peace Corps, [n.d.] 572p.

This volume consists of fifty lessons arranged in seven units of seven lessons each. The final lesson in each unit as well as the concluding lesson of the book are review lessons. Each lesson is constructed around a conversation or text that is based on real life experiences in Africa. An analysis section in each lesson discusses the application of the new grammar employed and provides 'drill' exercise. A Pidgin/English glossary is provided at the end of the volume.

152 **The languages of Africa.**
Joseph H. Greenberg. Bloomington, Indiana: Indiana University Press, 1963. 171p. 6 maps.

A basic, standard classification of African languages.

153 **Grammaire du Duala.** (Douala grammar.)
Johannes Ittmann, translated by L.A. Boumard. Douala,
Cameroon: Collège Libermann, 1978. 365p. bibliog.

This well organized grammatical text, intended for those interested in learning o
furthering their knowledge of Duala grammar, is organized in four main section
which provide the salient aspects of Duala phonetics, morphology, syntax, an
the derivation of words. Included are various tables of morphology and
'grammatical' index, listed alphabetically for easy reference, pertaining to specifi
grammatical questions or problems. The original German edition was published i
1939.

154 **Language usage in Cameroon urban centers.**
Stephen Jikong, Edna L. Koenig. In: *A sociolinguistic profile of
urban centers in Cameroon.* Edited by Edna L. Koenig, Emmanuel
Chia, John Povey. Los Angeles: Crossroads Press, 1983, p. 55-
77.

'With the complex linguistic situation in Cameroon, it is useful to know how the
members of this speech community communicate among themselves in the
presence of the various languages at their disposal.' In this article, the author
analyse data gathered in Cameroon urban centres.

155 **Sociolinguistic profile of the urban centers.**
Edna L. Koenig. In: *A sociolinguistic profile of urban centers in
Cameroon.* Edited by Edna L. Koenig, Emmanuel Chia, John
Povey. Los Angeles: Crossroads Press, 1983, p. 33-54. map.
bibliog.

Dr. Koenig presents the rationale and procedures of a linguistic survey which she
supervised in Cameroon urban centres. Basic data on language usage is analysed.

156 **A sociolinguistic profile of urban centers in Cameroon.**
Edited by Edna L. Koenig, Emmanuel Chia, John Povey, preface
by G. Richard Tucker, introduction by John Povey. Los Angeles:
Crossroads Press, 1983. 149p. map. bibliog.

This study was conducted by American and Cameroon scholars with the
assistance of students at the University of Yaoundé. In addition to the research
results, based on data gathered through survey research in several urban centres.
the volume contains an analysis and classification of Cameroon languages by
Emmanual Chia. Paul Mbangwana discusses the significant role of Pidgin English:
Gisèle Tchoungi examines the policy and the reality of bilingualism; and, Maurice
Tadadjeu suggests a variety of ideas on language planning studies. Cameroon is
an excellent location for the study of sociolinguistics, but relatively little research
has been conducted there. Of particular interest is the dynamic relations between
French and English, the two official languages, and between these and Pidgin
English, widely used in urban and southern rural areas.

157 The scope and role of Pidgin English in Cameroon.
Paul Nkad Mbangwana. In: *A sociolinguistic profile of urban centers in Cameroon*. Edited by Edna L. Koenig, Emmanuel Chia, John Povey. Los Angeles: Crossroads Press, 1983, p. 79-91. bibliog.

This article seeks to trace the historical path Pidgin English has traversed in Cameroon as one of the prototypes of a multilingual society. It also attempts to examine the various official attitudes expressed towards the use of Pidgin English *vis-a-vis* its actual use in daily life interactions.' The author concludes that Cameroon Pidgin English has become a true national language.

158 La situation linguistique du Cameroun 1. coup d'oeil sur les langues 2. aspects sociolinguistiques. (The Cameroon linguistic situation. 1. A glance at the languages 2. Sociolinguistic aspects.)
Patrick Renaud. In: *Inventaire des études linguistiques sur les pays d'Afrique noire d'expression Française et sur Madagascar*. Edited by D. Barreteau. Paris: Conseil International de Langue Française, 1978, p. 473-92. map. bibliog.

In this presentation of the linguistically diverse nature of Cameroon, the author first outlines and classifies Cameroon's numerous languages according to their linguistic families. A general overview and bibliography of major linguistic studies pertaining to Cameroon is included. This is followed by a brief analysis of sociolinguistic aspects of Cameroon, emphasizing the relationships between the various languages. A sociolinguistic bibliography is included and accompanied by other short bibliographies listing educational documents, works in national languages, sociolinguistic documents, and documents of linguistic politics.

159 First steps in Wes-Kos.
Gilbert D. Schneider. Hartford, Connecticut: Hartford Seminary Foundation, 1963. 81p. map. (Hartford Studies in Linguistics, no. 6).

This language manual is designed for adults who wish to learn Pidgin English and who already have a background in the English language. Introductory notes are followed by five chapters, each of which is divided into six sections. Firstly, conversations based on the type of Pidgin English one would hear and speak in West Cameroon, and especially in the highlands of West Cameroon, are presented. Cultural notes which elucidate the text are denoted and the structural forms necessary to communicate in Pidgin English and its sound system are described. Next, the various methods employed to form Pidgin English words and their classes are described and, finally, the English equivalents of special vocabulary words from the conversations are provided.

Languages

160 **A preliminary glossary: English-Pidgin-English (Wes-Kos).**
Gilbert D. Schneider, foreword by David B. Arnold.   Athens,
Ohio: Ohio University, Center for International Studies, 1965.
68p.

Pidgin English is the West African vernacular originating in the 18th century for
African peoples, coastal traders, and transient individuals who had no primary
language in common. The present glossary of Pidgin English vocabulary
indigenous to West Cameroon and Eastern Nigeria is the result of the author's
fourteen years (1946-1965) of living and working in the region. The glossary
provides Pidgin English equivalents of English vocabulary, which is arranged
alphabetically. The glossary includes a short introductory section describing
unique characteristics of Pidgin English.

161 **West African Pidgin-English: an historical overview.**
Gilbert D. Schneider.   Athens, Ohio: Ohio University, Center for
International Studies, 1967. 23p. (Papers in International Studies,
no. 8).

This historical overview of West African Pidgin English is the result of the
author's extensive field research in and personal knowledge of the area. The
historical evolution of the language and the foreign contributions to its expansion,
including Portuguese, British, Dutch, and German colonial interests, are explored
in this brief essay. Special emphasis is placed on the language's development in
the 19th century.

162 **Pidgin English proverbs.**
Gilbert D. Schneider.   East Lansing, Michigan: Michigan State
University, African Studies Center, [n.d.] 46p. (African Language
Monograph, no. 6).

The author provides a glossary of Pidgin English proverbs and their English
equivalents. Proverbs are a significant means of expression in Pidgin. A list of 110
Pidgin English 'work names' and their English equivalents is also included.

163 **Prospects for language planning studies in Cameroon.**
Maurice Tadajeu. In: *A sociolinguistic profile of urban centers in
Cameroon*. Edited by Edna L. Koenig, Emmanuel Chia, John
Povey.   Los Angeles: Crossroads Press, 1983, p. 117-24. bibliog.

The author defines several linguistic problems present in Cameroon and suggests
the role language planning might play in their solution.

164 **A grammar of the Adamawa dialect of the Fulani language.**
F. W. Taylor.   Oxford, England: Clarendon Press, 1953. 2nd ed.
124p.

The Fulani or Fulbe have for many years been politically dominant in much of
northern Cameroon.

165 **The languages of West Africa.**
Dietrich Westermann, M. A. Bryan.   Oxford, England: Oxford
University Press, 1952. 215p.
A standard classification system for West African languages.

A case for early bilingualism.
See item no. 395.

Focus on official bilingualism in Cameroon: its relationship to education.
See item no. 404.

Language, schools, and government in Cameroon.
See item no. 405.

Miscellany of Maroua Fulfulde (Northern Cameroon).
See item no. 439.

Bibliography of the Summer Institute of Linguistics, 1935-1975.
See item no. 501.

Religion

166 **One hundred years.**
Arthur Judson Brown, introduction by Charles R. Erdman. New
York, London: Fleming H. Revell Company, 1936. 1140p. maps.
This is a history of the foreign missionary work of the United States Presbyterian
Church by a writer who is noted for his studies of missionary problems. The
author was former secretary of the Board of Foreign Missions of the United
States Presbyterian Church. As a result of his extensive travel, the author
presents a personal account of the various nations that he has visited, the peoples
that live there, and the specific policies and problems of modern missions within
each nation. The American Presbyterian Mission was one of the earliest mission
groups to undertake activities in Cameroon. Its work centered on the
southeastern coastal area.

167 **Origine et développement d'une église indépendente Africaine:**
l'église Baptiste Camerounaise. (Origin and development of an
independent African church: the Cameroon Baptist church.)
Jean-René Brutsch. *Monde non Chrétien*, no. 12 (Oct-Dec.
1949), p. 408-24.
The author provides a brief overview of the historical origins and development of
the Cameroon Baptist Church. An annex to the article reproduces the statutes of
the church as published in the *Journal Officiel du Cameroun Française* on July 5,
1949. This church was organized and managed by Africans after the establishment
of German colonial rule.

168 **For the heart of Africa.**
Ruth Christiansen. Minneapolis, Minnesota: Augsburg
Publishing House, 1956. 271p. map.
The author served as a member of the Sudan Mission of the Evangelical Lutheran

56

Church, also known as the Gunderson Mission, in the northern parts of Francophone Cameroon. Poli, Rei Bouba, Meiganga, and Mboula were major centres of activity. This volume presents biographical material on the missionaries; geographical and ethnographic material on the region of activity; a historical discussion of the mission; and instructions to guide the activities of missionaries.

169 **An Englishwoman's twenty-five years in tropical Africa.**
George Hawker. London: Hodder & Stoughton, 1911. 352p.
map.

This study was commissioned by the Committee of the Baptist Missionary Society to preserve for posterity the works and travels of one of its missionaries, Mrs. Thomas Lewis. The author documents Mrs. Lewis' missionary work in the Cameroons, San Salvador Kibokolo, and Kimpese through a revealing presentation of the letters that she wrote during that time. Employing both extracts and narratives of her letters, a vivid description is made of her accomplishments and failures, the spread of the Baptist faith, and the nature of the lands she inhabited and the peoples she met. The volume 'will appeal strongly to all who are interested in the work of women, and in the Evangelisation of the world.'

170 **Sorcellerie, chimère dangereuse . . . ?** (Sorcery, dangerous
chimera . . . ?)
Meinrad P. Hebga. Abidjan: INADES, 1979. 301p. bibliog.

Sorcery, also known as witchcraft or 'ju-ju,' represents a significant, but poorly understood, aspect of African religion, social relations, and health care. Most discussions of this subject have been prepared by European authors – and frequently by Christian missions whose approach is often biased. Here is a study by a Cameroonian, himself a Christian, with extensive training in Catholic educational institutions. The work is based on several years of study, mostly in the Yaoundé region, and on comparisons with other areas of Africa. The first half of the volume is descriptive; it contains major sections on the position of sorcery and magic, and on the good and evil powers of sorcery. The second, and much briefer section, is an interpretation of sorcery and a discussion of the relation between sorcery and Christianity.

171 **'The beloved,' an Iowa boy in the jungles of Africa.**
Edited by John Frederick Hinkhouse. Fairfield, Iowa: Privately
published, 1909. 294p.

This book is a memorial to the missionary work carried out by Charles Warmer McCleary in the 'Kamerun District' of the West Africa Mission of the Presbyterian Church. His 'drum-name . . . the one by which he was known from Batanga to Elat, was "The Beloved".' The volume studies the life, letters, and work of McCleary and also contains tributes by Dr. A. W. Halsey, Dr. Orville Reed, and Rev. Melvin Fraser. A perusal of McCleary's correspondence with his family provides the reader with the problems, prospects, and rewards of missionary work, as well as the customs, mores, and day-to-day living experiences of the peoples with whom McCleary interacted.

Religion

172 **The Cameroons and the Baptist mission in four parts.**
Alexander Innes. Birkenhead, England: the author, 1895. 2nd ed. 73p.

Writing in a polemic fashion, the author attacks the despotic nature of the Baptist Missionary Society in general and that of Alfred Saker, who was one of the missionaries, in particular. Innes wishes to completely refute various statements made in the *Centenary Volume* of the Baptist Missionary Society. The first half of the book is dedicated to a refutation of the *Centenary Volume* and a verification of the cruelties reportedly committed by Saker in Cameroon as seen by eyewitnesses. The second half documents the embezzlement of funds from the society and the further exposure of atrocities committed in Cameroon (such as the flogging of women and the hanging of African soldiers). A petition is presented which calls upon the British Parliament to establish a court of justice to put down further atrocities.

173 **The life of Rowland Hill Evans of Cameroon.**
E. Edwin Jones. Columbus, Ohio: the author, 1932. 219p. map.

Evans was a member of the West Africa Mission of the Presbyterian Church (USA) in Cameroon from 1909 until his death in 1932. Along with the rest of this mission, most of his work was carried out in the South Eastern part of the country, especially Lolodorf, Efulan, and Elat. He played an important part in the training of African pastors, particularly during his brief reign as President of Dager Biblical Seminary. While the majority of the volume discusses Evans' life and work, useful descriptive material on Cameroon life and society and on the history of his mission is included. A hand-drawn map shows the locations in the 1920s of Presbyterian communion and evangelist locations between Lolodorf, the Ntem River, the Ocean, and Sangmelima. The volume also contains several photographs.

174 **The history of the Presbyterian Church in West Cameroon.**
Werner Keller. Buea, Cameroon: Radio and Literature Department of the Presbyterian Church, 1969. 154p. map. bibliog.

The author provides a survey of the general development of the Presbyterian Church in Cameroon up to 1960. Included is a chronological analysis of the origins of the church, the spread of missionary schools, the trend towards self-determination and church autonomy, and the various branches of church and mission work. Three additional chapters written by J. Schnellback, Ernst Schmidt and J. R. Brutsch update the development of the church to 1968. Special topics include an analysis of the development of the Presbyterian Church of East Cameroon and the integration into a single unified structure of the previously separate church organizations of East and West Cameroon.

175 **The discipling of West Cameroon: a study of Baptist growth.**
Lloyd Emerson Kwast, foreword by Donald McGavran. Grand Rapids, Michigan: William B. Eerdmands Publishing Company, 1971. 205p. 6 maps. bibliog.

The author provides a historical analysis of the rise of the Baptist Church in West or anglophone Cameroon. The study begins with an examination of the

geographic, ethnic, linguistic, political, and religious environment of West
Cameroon. It goes on to present both a historical and statistical view of the
growth of the church, emphasizing the social and religious factors which have
fostered this growth. Finally, a general view is provided of the other churches of
West Cameroon, mission policy, and 'planning boldly' for the continued growth
of the Baptist Church in the region.

176 **Contribution á l'étude du comportement religieux des Wodaabe
      Dageeja du Nord-Cameroun.** (Contribution to the study of the
      religious behaviour of North Cameroon's Wodaabe Dageeja.)
      Robert Labatut. *Journal des Africanistes*, vol. 48, no. 2 (1978), p.
      63-92.
The first half of the article describes the Islamic faith, the way it is practiced and
taught, and the forms it has taken at important periods in the life and culture of
the Wodaabe Dageeja, a group of North Cameroon Peul nomads. The second
half of the article provides observations, and documents the Wodaabe Dageeja's
pre-Islamic religious background. Factors discussed include myths of origin, rites
concerning fire, the cow, transhumance, important annual feasts, spirits, magical
practices, and the symbolism of black and white.

177 **These seventy years: an autobiography.**
      Thomas Lewis.   London: Carey Press, 1930. 300p. 3 maps.
Thomas Lewis was an early member of the Saker Baptist Mission which played
such an important role in the pre-colonial history of Christianity in Cameroon,
particularly in the areas of Victoria, Bimbia, and Douala. Lewis arrived at
Victoria in 1883 and departed from Cameroon in 1886 to serve his mission
elsewhere in Africa. Most of this volume discusses his later work, but there are
useful chapters describing Victoria and its inhabitants and the German takeover
of Cameroon. The Baptist Mission was intricately involved in that takeover.

178 **Black sheep, adventures in West Africa.**
      Jean Kenyon Mackenzie.   Boston; New York: Houghton Mifflin,
      1916. 314p.
This volume comprises a collection of letters written by the author, who was a
member of the American Presbyterian Mission of Southern Cameroon from 1904
to 1913. These letters, had 'no other aim than that common effort of exiles – the
daily renewing, by the expense of spirit in a letter, of the dearest companion-
ships.' However, these letters play another role in that they trace the rise of the
Presbyterian faith in Cameroon, whose first inland station was opened in 1893.
The author speaks approvingly of this 'great experience,' noting how the advance
of the faith facilitated the indigenization of the religion under 'black leaders.' The
letters are divided in story-form into four major sections; mail from the bush, mail
from the new clearing, mail from the beach, and the harvest mail. They provide a
valuable description of the peoples and environment of the Kribi, Elat and
Ebolowa areas.

179 **An African trail.**
Jean Kenyon Mackenzie. West Medford, Massachusetts: Central
Committee on the United Study of Foreign Missions, 1917. 222p.
bibliog.

The Central Committee originally commissioned this work as 'a text-book on the
approach of the Gospel to primitive peoples'. In essence, the work portrays the
ways in which religion has influenced the lives of the Bulu people of Cameroon.
The first two chapters denote the general role of the missionary in Africa and the
general characteristics of the Bulu. Subsequent chapters examine the role of God
in Bulu society, 'The ten tyings' (ten commandments), 'The new tribe' (converts),
and 'The New Custom' (practices of the faith).

180 **The Catholic Church in Kom: its foundation and growth,
1913-1977.**
Paul Nchoji Nkwi, foreword by Monsignor Paul
Verdzekov. Yaoundé: Afo-A-Kom Publications, 1977. 23p.

This booklet was written to commemorate the Golden Jubilee of the establishment of Njinikom Parish (1927-1977). The author's purpose is to 'pinpoint the
landmarks of the Catholic Church in Kom.' The first section details the period
1913-1926 preceding the creation of Njinikom Parish. Mention is made of the
arrival of the first German missionaries, their creation of Fujua Parish and its
subsequent removal to Njinikom, and the Christian-Fon conflict. The second
section presents a chronological sequence of events which portray the rise and
spread of the Catholic faith in Kom. This is one of the very few microlevel studies
of Christianity in Cameroon.

181 **Journey in faith: the story of the Presbyterian Church in
Cameroon.**
Edited by Reverend Nyansako-ni-Nku. Yaoundé: Buma Kor,
1982. 173p.

This collection, published in honour of the Silver Jubilee of the Presbyterian
Church in anglophone Cameroon, contains twenty brief essays by leading
members of the Church. These essays are separated into three subjects:
evangelism; social services; and 'Life and work: the Church with God's people.'
The latter section considers church organization. Several of the contributors are
well-known in other spheres of life – S. T. Muna has been Prime Minister of West
Cameroon and Victor Mukete was Chairman of the Cameroon Development
Corporation. This volume is more a description of the activities of the Church
today than a history.

182 **Out of the African night.**
William D. Rayburn. New York, London: Harper & Row, 1968.
176p.

This is the story of a medical mission written in the form of a series of episodes
spanning nearly half a century. The author claims to 'depict accurately and
interestingly the revealing events in the lives of Africans which will help the
reader to gain an understanding of the response of one small part of Africa

(Southern Cameroon) to modern medicine.' Chapters which are representative of the general flavour of the book include 'Surgery vs. witchcraft,' 'A prayer and a dentist's chair,' 'Termites and tsetse flies,' and 'Gunpoint surgery.'

183   **Alfred Saker: the pioneer of the Cameroons.**
      E. M. Saker.   London: Religious Tract Society, 1908. 224p.
      map.

This biography of Alfred A. Saker, a Baptist missionary in Cameroon, was written by his daughter, E. M. Saker. An account is made of Saker's youth, his initial call to the Baptist faith as a minister, his first experiences in Africa, and final settlement in Cameroon. Saker's daughter writes of his contributions to the spread of the Baptist faith in Cameroon, the perils encountered by early missionary outposts, and his travels throughout the territory. A supplementary chapter, entitled 'Appendix', was written by Edward B. Underhill and it describes Saker's ascent of Mount Cameroon (1861-1862).

184   **Histoire de l'église en Afrique (Cameroun).** (History of the Church
      in Africa (Cameroon).)
      Jaap Van Slageren.   Yaoundé: Editions CLE, 1969. 149p. 10
      maps.

This volume is the sixth in a series which is designed to present various topics in religious studies for the secondary school student. The book contains twenty-five lessons pertaining to the history of Christianity in Africa. The first six chapters discuss the history of the Church in Africa in general. The rest of the book is devoted to a more precise historical study of Protestant missions in Cameroon. The role and influence of foreign Protestant missions emanating from Germany, France, Switzerland, Norway, and the United States is presented, with a small annex devoted to the role of Catholic missions in Cameroon.

185   **Les origines de l'église évangélique du Cameroun: missions**
      Européennes et Christianisme autochtone. (Origins of the
      Evangelical Church in Cameroon: European missions and native
      Christianity.)
      Jaap Van Slageren.   Leiden, Netherlands: Brill, 1972. 297p. 4
      maps. bibliog.

This work traces the general advance of the Evangelical Church in Cameroon from its origins to its proclamation of autonomy in 1975. The author analyses the rise of Christianity in the pre-colonial era (1841-1886) and its subsequent expansion into the interior during the period of German colonial rule (1886-1902). A special section traces the reactions of the peoples of the Grassfields to the rising tide of Christianity. A detailed analysis is made of the missionary movement and the rise of an indigenously supported Christian faith. The entire movement is marked by and culminated in a general evolution towards autonomy for the Evangelical Church.

Religion

186 **The words of God in an African forest.**
W. Reginald Wheeler, forword by Jean Kenyon Mackenzie. New
York, London: Fleming H. Revell, 1931. 318p. 2 maps. bibliog.

One of many reports by Americans who worked with the American Presbyterian
Mission in Central Africa. This Mission was in Cameroon almost from the
beginnings of German colonial rule and continues to work in the country today.
The Mission and its efforts were located entirely in the francophone part of the
country and operated separately from the Presbyterian Mission (the Basel
Mission) in the anglophone sector. The memoirs and written reports of these
missionaries are an important source of information on life in Cameroon at the
end of the 19th century, as well as on the history of the Christian churches in
Cameroon.

In French Cameroons, Bandjoon.
See item no. 37.

**Histoire des forces religieuses au Cameroon: de la première guerre
mondiale à l'indépendence (1916-1955).** (History of religious forces in
Cameroon: from the First World War to independence (1916-1955).)
See item no. 130.

Islamic law in Africa.
See item no. 295.

Population, Health and Welfare

187 **Divorce and fertility: an African study.**
Edwin Ardener.   London: Oxford University Press, 1962. 171p.
(Nigerian Social and Economic Studies, no. 3).
This study, which centres on the Victoria Division of Cameroon, was intended as
a smaller comparison to *Plantation and village in the Cameroons* (q.v.). Ardener
first discusses the marital variable from his sample of 1,000 interviews with women
in terms of several other variables such as, age structure, religious affiliation and
education. Secondly, a close examination is made of marital stability in relation to
other variables including, religion of the woman and her partner, and occupation.
Finally the role of fertility and the women's reasons for divorce are explicated.

188 **Budgets familiaux des planteurs de cacao au Cameroun.** (Family
budgets of Cameroon cocoa planters.)
Jacques Binet, preface by Hubert Deschamps.   Paris: ORSTOM,
1956. 154p. 4 maps. (L'Homme d'Outre-mer, no. 3).
The purpose of this study is to examine the impact on the family of the movement
from a subsistence economy to one which is monetary in nature. Results are
gleaned from an analysis of the family budgets of cocoa planters in Cameroon.
The study takes into account the various aspects of the economic life of the cocoa
planters, including migrations and the established social order, the dispersion and
absence of commerce, demography, the influence of schools and missions, and the
matrimonial statute. Family expenditures, savings, and the diverse sources of
revenues are examined both individually and in relation to the way they affect
each other.

189   **Main results of the April 1976 general population and housing census.**
Cameroon. Ministry of Economic Affairs and Planning, 1978. 33p.
3 maps.

This booklet is an extremely useful and concise publication for obtaining quick information concerning the main aspects of Cameroon's *1976 general population and housing census*. Simplified sections entitled 'How was our census conducted?' 'How many are we in Cameroon?', 'What do we do?', and 'How do we live?', present statistical information in both chart and graph form. An appendix provides population figures for each province, division, and subdivision. This is a much abbreviated version of the published census reports.

190   **The population of West Cameroon: main findings of the 1964 demographic sample survey.**
Cameroon. Ministry of Economic Affairs and Planning.
Department of Statistics; Paris: Société d'Etudes pour le
Développement Economique et Social, 1965. 297p. 5 maps.

This report presents the preliminary results of a demographic survey conducted in anglophone Cameroon in 1963. A brief introduction to the history and geography of West Cameroon is followed by an analysis of the population. Major topics include ethnicity; migration; demographic structure; school attendance; local trade, crafts and skills; and the nomadic population. The final results of the survey were published in a two-volume set (plus a summary volume) in 1969, *La population du Cameroun occidental*. (Paris: Secrétariat d'Etat aux Affaires Etrangères, 1969).

191   **United Republic of Cameroon national nutrition survey.**
Cameroon Government, with University of California Nutrition
Assessment Unit, United States Agency for International
Development.   Washington DC: USAID, 1978. 387p. 6 maps.
bibliog.

This report is the result of collaboration between the Government of Cameroon, the University of California Nutrition Assessment Unit (UCLA), and the United States Agency for International Development (USAID). The key objectives and results of the estimates survey are of the nutritional status of young children and their mothers, comparisons of nutritional status among selected areas, and an examination of factors which affect this status, that is, diet, socioeconomic factors, health and demographic variables. Extensive appendixes provide the research design of the study, survey analysis, anthropometric reference data, methods and procedures, and additional survey results.

64

92   **Recensement général de la population et de l'habitat d'avril 1976.**
      (General census of the population and living conditions in April
      1976.)
      Cameroun. Ministère de l'Economie et du Plan. Direction de la
      Statistique et de la Comptabilité Nationale.   Yaoundé: Bureau
      Central du Recensement, 1978. 4 vols. maps.

The results of the first real national census of Cameroon have been published in
four volumes which cover results, analysis, cities and villages, and general
discussion, though each volume consists of several 'tomes' or books, forming a
total of twenty-two books. This is the most reliable analysis of Cameroon's
population, though there are persistent rumours that some figures for the overall
population have been altered for political purposes.

93   **Population distribution and dynamics in Cameroon.**
      John I. Clarke. In: *Kamerun*. Edited by Hans F. Illy.   Mainz,
      GFR: Hase & Koehler Verlag, 1974, p. 13-35. 9 maps. bibliog.

Cameroon population distribution and dynamics are not unusual, but are
frequently characterized by a combination of traditional and modern elements.
Discrepancies in regional rates of population increase will decline, but the high
rate of migration will continue, possibly leading to increases in unemployment
and underemployment.

94   **Societal causes of infertility and population decline among the
      settled Fulani of North Cameroon.**
      N. David, V. David.   *Man*, vol. 16, no. 4 (1981), p. 644-64.

An account of the numerous societal causes of infertility and population decline
and the way in which they interact with one another.

95   **Wage earner and mother: compatibility of roles on a Cameroon
      plantation.**
      Virginia DeLancey. In: *Women, education and modernization of
      the family*. Edited by Helen Ware.   Canberra: Australian National
      University, 1981, p. 1-21. bibliog. (Changing African Family
      Project, Monograph no. 7).

The primary purpose of this study is to determine whether or not wage-employed
women exhibit compatibility or incompatibility between their roles as wage
employees and as mothers. The sample for the study was drawn from wage
earning women living with their husbands on the Tole Tea Estates on the
Cameroon Development Corporation in the Southwest Province of Cameroon.
The general conclusion of the study is that 'under the relatively favourable
conditions provided by the Cameroon Development Corporation personnel
policies and the government labor and social insurance legislation, it is possible
for female employees to work for wages outside their homes and away from the
families without having unsolvable problems of role compatibility.'

196   **Inhabited space in Elog-Mpoo country.**
Cosem Dikoume.   *African Environment* (Dakar), vol. 4, no. 1
(1980), p. 27-37.

The article describes housing and land allocation systems in the low-population
density area of Elog-Mpoo.

197   **A Cameroon village seeks animal protein.**
Peter Efange, J. N. Ikundi. In: *Growing out of poverty*. Edited by
Elizabeth Stamp.   Oxford, England: Oxford University Press,
1977, p. 94-107. map.

The authors discuss a multifaceted plan for rural development executed in the
Bakweri village of Small Soppo, with special emphasis on the role of Oxfam in the
project.

198   **Cameroon: the interrelation of population and development.**
Futures Group, Resources for the Awareness of Population
Impacts on Development (RAPID).   Washington, DC: Futures
Group, 1983. 33p. bibliog.

This is one of a series of reports on the 'Resources for the Awareness of
Population Impacts on Development' (RAPID) project. The primary goal of the
study as related to Cameroon is to show the distinct relationship between
population growth and socioeconomic development. Short essays on various
topics such as 'age distribution and child dependency,' 'momentum of population
growth,' and 'fertility, infertility, and population growth' are followed by a
graphic representation in the form of charts or figures. The study examines
numerous development goals according to two basic research questions: firstly, if
the present high level of fertility is continued, what will be the effect on the ability
of Cameroon to attain its economic and social development goals?; and secondly,
how much difference would it make if the development programme included
measures to slow down population growth?

199   **The Cameroons and Togoland: a demographic study.**
Robert R. Kuczynski.   London, New York: Oxford University
Press for the Royal Institute of International Affairs, 1939. 579p. 4
maps. bibliog.

This is the most authoritative study of the Cameroon population for the period
from the beginning of colonial rule until just prior to the Second World War.
There are sections on German, British, and French Cameroons. The research was
based on thorough analysis of statistical material collected by colonial authorities,
though such statistics do leave much to be desired. In each section Kuczynski
examines African and European populations; census and other statistical
material; fertility, mortality, and population growth; and 'special investigations.'
He argues that German analyses of population were inaccurate, but the
conclusions they reached were correct, in that there probably was little population
growth in the German period. He condemns the French for their failure to collect
adequate population information. The British collected more data, but it was
inaccurate and no determination of growth or decrease was possible.

66

200 **A benefit-cost analysis of measles vaccinations in Yaoundé, Cameroon.**
William Martin Makinen. Ann Arbor, Michigan: University of Michigan, Center for Research on Economic Development, November 1981. 20p. (Discussion paper, no. 96).

Contributes to an understanding of public health programmes in general and more specifically that of measles vaccination in Cameroon in three ways: 'to contribute to the rationalization of the decision-making process for the allocation of resources to health programs; to examine the methodology currently used to evaluate the economic merits of health programs; and to present a methodology for application to the anti-measle vaccination programme in Yaoundé, Cameroon.'

201 **L'Existence au Cameroun.** (Life in Cameroon.)
Gustave Martin, preface by M. Le Dr. Calmette. Paris: Emile Larose, 1921. 533p. 7 maps.

The main aim of this volume is to provide an overview of health and medical conditions in French Cameroon in the 1920s and to discover their potential effect on the various colonial administrators, on the armed forces, the businessmen, and the religious personnel living and working there. Firstly, the book describes the 'medical geography' and 'pathology' of Cameroon. Secondly, the 'noseography,' or description and classification of diseases present in Cameroon, is methodically discussed. Thirdly, personal hygiene and the protection of public health is outlined, and fourthly, the organization of health services in the colony is described. The volume concludes with a section entitled 'Advice to Europeans'; in short, general rules of personal hygiene for all Europeans thinking of traveling to Cameroon.

202 **Health and medicine. The economic potential of West Cameroon, priorities for development, vol. 2.**
James G. Roney. Menlo Park, California: Stanford Research Institute, 1965. 51p. 2 maps.

Health problems, health facilities, and health personnel and their training are described in this study. Recommendations for improved health care are also presented.

203 **Family life and structure in Southern Cameroon.**
Winifred Weekes Vagliani, Manga Bekombo, Lynn Wallisch. Paris: Development Centre of the Organisation for Economic Co-operation and Development, 1976. 87p. 6 maps. bibliog.

The purpose of this study is to examine, in three areas of Southern Cameroon, the effect that three modernizing variables (education, employment, and type and place of settlement) have on the family and the family structure. This single national study was part of a much larger programme entitled 'The International Project on the Changing African Family' which was to include twenty to twenty-five additional nations. The objective data incorporated into the study includes the size and composition of households, the economic obligations of family members, and fertility or the number of live births. Subjective data incorporated into the study explicated individual opinions and attitudes toward traditional family customs, family life, desired fertility, the value of education, and perception of the outside world.

204   **Some explanations of high fertility among rural women in Cameroon.**
Winifred Weekes Vagliani. In: *The persistence of high fertility.* Edited by J. C. Caldwell.   Canberra: Australian National University, 1977, p. 451-66.

The primary factors sustaining high fertility in Southern Cameroon are said to be the economic autonomy of most rural women and the extended family. The present article analyses the variable of education as a potential factor in changing the traditional cultural values related to fertility and family structure among Southern Cameroon women. The author first provides background information on the women concerning marital status, age at marriage or first birth, sources of income, economic responsibility, and living arrangements. A description is subsequently made of women's attitudes to relationships between males and females; desired fertility; and polygyny, family structure and fertility.

Code du travail: labour code.
See item no. 296.

Législation Camerounaise du travail. (Cameroon labour legislation.)
See item no. 304.

Pilot study on social criteria for development cooperation.
See item no. 358.

Plantation workers: conditions of work and standards of living.
See item no. 359.

Demographic Yearbook.
See item no. 457.

Urbanization and Migration

205 **Plantation and village in the Cameroons.**
Edwin Ardener, Shirley Ardener, W. A. Warmington,
introduction by J. Henry Richardson, preface by E. M.
Chilver. London: Oxford University Press for the Nigerian
Institute of Social and Economic Research, 1960. 435p. 6 maps.
The German plantations around Mt. Cameroon were eventually taken over by the
British colonial authorities to form the Cameroons Development Corporation.
This remains the largest employer after the bureaucracy in the country. Most of
the employees are migrants, and concern has frequently been expressed about the
effects of such massive migration on both society and the individuals. This study
was an attempt to analyse those effects. The report is presented in three
parts – the employers and life at the plantations, the home or labour source areas,
and the populations of the plantation zone. Marriage and prostitution,
agriculture, migration, diet and health, ethnic composition of the labour force,
and expenditure patterns of migrants are among the many topics. The two source
areas selected for study were Esu in Bamenda and the Banyang in the forest area.
This is an important and valuable study and its conclusions should be considered
for any research of a sociological nature in anglophone Cameroon.

206 **Cameroun: l'exode rural.** (Cameroon: the rural exodus.)
Haman Bako. *Journal of African Marxists*, no. 5 (Feb. 1984),
p. 51-76.
Summarizes the causes and effects of migration to the cities of Cameroon, using a
Marxist model as the basis of analysis.

69

207   **Un espace de migrations frontalières importantes, le Nord-Cameroun.** (North Cameroon: an area of important transfrontier migration.)
      A. Beauvilain.   *Cahiers Géographiques de Rouen*, vol. 15 (1981), p. 35-46. map.
Colonial boundaries near Lake Chad cut across traditional pastoral migration routes. A fuller discussion of migration in North Cameroon is contained in 'Les migrations' by J. Boutrais, G. Pontie, Y. Marguerat and A. Beauvilain in *Le nord du Cameroun: des hommes, une région*, (Paris: ORSTOM, 1984), p. 305-74.

208   **L'Espace commercial des Bamiléké.** (Commercial space of the Bamileke.)
      Jacques Champaud.   *Espace Géographique*, vol. 10, no. 3 (1981), p. 198-206. map.
Bamileke migration to urban and rural sites has been an important aspect of their rise to commercial and agricultural importance in Cameroon. They have integrated traditional social structures with the modern commercial system to bring about this success.

209   **Villes et campagnes du Cameroon de l'Ouest.** (The towns and countryside of West Cameroon.)
      Jacques Champaud.   Paris: Editions de l'ORSTOM, 1983. 508p.
The author, a noted writer on the rural geography of West Cameroon, provides a comprehensive survey of the cities and countryside of this region. Rural-urban migration is examined.

210   **Social change and sexual differentiation in the Cameroun and Ivory Coast.**
      Remi Clignet.   *Signs: Journal of Women in Culture and Society*, vol. 3, no. 1 (Autumn 1977), p. 244-60.
The article examines the independence and complementarity of two hypotheses concerning social change and sexual differentiation. The first states that 'the extent and form of sexual inequalities may depend primarily upon the complexity of social structures and hence upon the growth of schools, cities, and modern enterprises.' The second states that 'sexual inequalities may also depend on past and present cultural models and stereotypes.' The author first provides a general overview of Cameroon and the Ivory Coast, subsequently analysing the participation of women in educational structures and the relationships of urbanization and employment to sexual differentiation.

211   **The urban development of Buea: an essay in social geography.**
      Georges Courade.   Yaoundé: ORSTOM, 1972. 27p. 3 maps.
This booklet provides a brief overview of the towns in the Fako Division (Buea) and their environmental milieu. The main sections briefly describe the nature, history, and people in the formation of Buea, the development of the urban area, and the different areas in Buea. Two appendixes provide a methodological note

enoting the method of using administrative census and a key to the various maps resented. The author is a French geographer with several years of research xperience in Cameroon.

12 **Victoria, Bota: urban growth and immigration.**
Georges Courade, translated by Jeanne le Foll-Jacob.   Yaoundé: ORSTOM-ONAREST, 1976. 94p.

oday, Victoria, which was built on government land around shops and dministrative buildings, and Bota, which was built on land belonging to the main ociety of commercial plantations, now the Cameroon Development Corporation, rm a single urban unit. This volume attempts to describe why Victoria/Bota has ot grown at a rate commensurate wth other 'political capital cities' in Central frica since 1960. Furthermore, an attempt is made to describe the moderate opulation growth which has taken place, despite the fact that as an urban centre lacks 'dynamism' with respect to local employment possibilities. The author rms this situation as 'growth without development.'

13 **Plantation and migration in the Mt. Cameroon region.**
Mark W. DeLancey. In: *Kamerun.* Edited by Hans F. Illy.   Mainz, GFR: Hase and Koehler Verlag, 1974, p. 181-236.

he plantations around Mt. Cameroon were started by the Germans and remain oday as a major economic structure of the Cameroon government. Except for the overnment bureaucracy, the plantations are the largest employer in the country. igration to these estates has been a significant socioeconomic factor, especially anglophone Cameroon, since the 1890s. Here, DeLancey investigates changes migration patterns with special reference to ethnic factors.

14 **Migrants in voluntary associations in a rural setting: the case of the Cameroon Development Corporation.**
Mark W. DeLancey.   Pittsburgh, Pennsylvania: International Studies Association, Comparative Interdisciplinary Studies Section, 1974. 35p. (Working Paper, no. 41).

ased on survey research conducted in Cameroon, the author attempts to escribe and analyse the effects of multiethnic membership of voluntary ssociations on ethnocentrism.

15 **The competitive migration fields of Douala and Yaoundé, Cameroon.**
Jean-Louis Dongmo. In: *Redistribution of population in Africa.* Edited by J. I. Clarke, (et al.).   Nairobi: Heinemann, 1982, p. 133-37. 5 maps.

most African nations there exists a political and economic capital which ominates all other cities in gross population. The primary reason for this is the ajor city's attraction of 'rural exodus.' Cameroon is unusual, however, in that it as both an economic capital (Douala) and a political capital (Yaoundé). The ompetitive migrational attractions of these two cities are compared in this article. n analysis is made of the basic conditions of 'out-migration' toward Douala and

71

Yaoundé and the role that the two cities play as receivers of migration. The author, a Cameroonian, is a geography professor at the University of Yaoundé.

216 **Ikpe migrant cocoa farmers in South-West Cameroun: causes, problems and prospects.**
Stephen Ekpenyong. *Africa*, vol. 54, no. 1 (1984), p. 20-30.

The general conclusion of this study is that the large-scale migration of agricultural workers from Ikpe villages in Nigeria to the cocoa plantations in South-West Cameroon 'is the outcome of a maldistribution of population in relation to natural resources in south-eastern Nigeria.' A brief analysis is made of the problems and prospects of this migration.

217 **Migrational changes in West Cameroon.**
Emmanuel Gwan. In: *Redistribution of population in Africa.* Edited by J. I. Clarke, (et al.). Nairobi: Heinemann, 1980, p. 124-32. bibliog. 5 maps.

This is an excellent brief analysis of migrational movements and changes in anglophone Cameroon. After discussing pre-colonial mass migrations, the article studies 'forced' migrations during the German colonial era and 'individually motivated' migrations during the British colonial era. The individually motivated migrations discussed include those of nomadic Fulani migrants, migrant fishermen, plantation labour movements, and agricultural settlers. Finally, the role of urbanization and the general effects of population movements are described. Effects of migrations are discussed in terms of intermarriage, vital rates, sex ratios, labour force dependency, and age-sex structure.

218 **Confrontation and incorporation: Igbo ethnicity in Cameroon.**
Gerald W. Kleis. *African Studies Review*, vol. 23, no. 3 (Dec. 1980), p. 89-100. bibliog.

Although there are more striking manifestations of ethnicity in rural than in urban areas, an analysis of Igbo migrants in the village, 'conforms to the model of an ethnic group defined in terms of cohesion and corporate activity.' Corporate activity within the rural areas is said to result from various interrelated factors such as small group size, homogeneity, the nature of the rural economy, and frequent interaction with fellow Igbos. The author shows that in contrast to the confrontational ethnicity of the town, ethnicity in the village is nonconfrontational or integrative. The Igbos in Cameroon are recent arrivals from Nigeria. Their presence in Cameroon has caused antagonism and has been a focus of anglophone discontent.

219 **Profile of a commercial town in West-Cameroon.**
C. S. I. J. Lagerberg, G. J. Wilms. Tilburg, Netherlands: Tilburg University Press, 1974. 76p. 5 maps.

The authors present an in-depth study of the size, composition and growth of the populations of the Kumba urban districts of Fiango, Haussa, 3-corners, and Kumba-Town. The purpose of the study is to shed light on the sociological occurrence of urbanization and its subsequent problems of unemployment migration, education, and others. The methodology employed is that of 'clustered area-sampling' because of the paucity of official vital statistics available at the time of the study. The volume suffers from poor editing and problems in research and interpretation.

220 **Le rôle de la femme dans l'économie urbaine à Douala.** (The role of the woman in the urban economy of Douala.)
Guy Mainet. *Annalles de la Faculté des Lettres et des Sciences Humaines* (1979), p. 187-204.
Provides an analysis of women's role in the economy of Douala.

221 **Analyse numérique des migrations vers les villes du Cameroun.** (Numerical analysis of migrations to the cities of Cameroon.)
Y. Marguerat. Yaoundé: ORSTOM, 1973. 161p. 34 maps. (Travaux et Documents de l'ORSTOM, no. 40).
In this quantitative study of rural/urban migration in Cameroon, a general analysis is made of the 'rural exodus' and the reasons for urban attraction. Second, the author presents 'numerical confrontations' or tests of several propositions and hypotheses. Various factors, including 'rural density,' 'scolarization' and 'accessibility,' are tested to determine their impact on urban migration.

222 **Douala: un siècle en images.** (Douala: a century in pictures.)
Jacques Soulillou. Paris: the author, 1982. 120p. 10 maps. bibliog.
The author presents an illustrated history of Douala utilizing drawings and photographs to document the changes and development of the city from 1860 to 1955. Two major sections depict the development of Douala from 1860-1914 and 1920-1955. An interesting section depicts the 'itinerary,' or attractions that a traveller to Douala would encounter in 1949. A highly descriptive text is accompanied by over one hundred black and white drawings and photographs.

223 **Urbanization and population redistribution: trends in Cameroon.**
Lucas Tandap. In: *Redistribution of population in Africa.* Edited by J. I. Clarke, (et al.). Nairobi: Heinemann, 1982, p. 138-45. 5 maps.
Cameroon's population is largely concentrated in the South, West and North. The purpose of this article is 'to evaluate the role of the urbanization trend as a factor in the progressive redistribution of the population of Cameroon.' By examining economic and politico-administrative factors as determinants of urbanization and population redistribution, trends which are said to be enhanced by the presence of a social and welfare service infrastructure, distinct patterns are extrapolated which enable tentative projections of the future population distribution of Cameroon.

Health and disease on the plantations of Cameroon, 1884-1939.
See item no. 95.

Politics and Administration

224 Contribution to national construction.
Ahmadou Ahidjo. Paris: Présence Africaine, 1964. 136p.
(African Political Leaders).

The text is former president Ahmadou Ahidjo's outline as presented at the Maroua Party Congress in 1962 for dealing with all internal and external problems that could hinder the development of the Cameroon nation. The work is important in that it represents the early solidification of President Ahidjo's political views. The major topics dealt with are home, foreign, economic, social, and financial policies, and 'self-decolonisation.' The volume is also available in French.

225 Nation and development in unity and justice.
Ahmadou Ahidjo. Paris: Présence Africaine, 1969. 94p.

This volume, which is also available in French, contains the text of Ahidjo's address to the First Congress of the Cameroon National Union held in Garoua in 1969. As such, it stands as an important review of the accomplishments of the Ahidjo régime and its plans for the future. *See also* no. 242.

226 Fondements et perspectives du Cameroun nouveau. (Foundations and perspectives of the new Cameroon.)
Ahmadou Ahidjo. Aubagne-en-Provence, France: Saint Lambert Editeur, 1976. 181p.

This volume presents the plan of action for the party and the state for the five years which had passed since the first congress of the Cameroon National Union (CNU). Ahidjo discusses the 'révolution pacifique du 20 Mai 1972,' national independence and nonalignment, the efficacity of the CNU, social justice and the protection of workers, and the need for 'revolutionary reform.' Also examined are the desired courses of action in various functional fields such as agriculture, industry and infrastructure, finances, and the social and cultural realms. This limited edition was sold to raise funds for the Party as much as to inform Party members.

27 **Paul Biya ou l'incarnation de rigueur.** (Paul Biya or the incarnation of rigour.)
Edited by Jean Fouman Akawe, preface by Ahmadou
Ahidjo. Yaoundé: University of Yaoundé, 1983. 293p. 2 maps.

This is the first biographical work published pertaining to Paul Biya, the second president of Cameroon. The book traces Biya's life from his roots in Mvomeka'a, his scholastic career including time spent at Saint Joseph's Seminary, Lycée Leclerc, and the University of Paris, culminating in his involvement in politics and administration in Cameroon. The study provides a full explanation of Biya's political philosophy and his views on life in general. An extensive appendix reproduces nine of Biya's more memorable speeches.

28 **Political conflicts within the traditional and the modern institutions of the Bafut-Cameroon.**
Michael Tabuwe Aletum, preface by Albert
Doutreloux. Louvain, Belgium: Vander, 1974. 175p. 3 maps. bibliog.

An analysis and illumination of the types of conflict within traditional political institutions among the Bafut people. It is hypothesized that these conflicts have led to more general conflicts between modern and traditional Bafut political institutions. The author asserts that 'sound economic development' depends on 'social stability' while 'sound political development' depends on 'social understanding' between individuals within a political territorial unit. Development can thus only come about by understanding and attempting to settle the inherent conflicts between traditional and modern political institutions. The author, a Cameroonian and a member of the Bafut society, has based this work, originally a PhD dissertation, on field work and on the analysis of previously published materials. He did not utilize archival resources.

29 **Les chemins de l'unité: comment se forge une nation, l'exemple Camerounais.** (The paths of unity: how to forge a nation, Cameroon example)
Jos-Blaise Alima. Paris: Afrique Biblio Club, 1977. 2nd ed. 184p. bibliog.

The author, one of the best known Cameroonian journalists, describes the forging of a nation through the example of Cameroon. The first two sections of the book examine historically salient points of Cameroon's recent past, the rise of Cameroon nationalism, the UPC rebellion, and the fight for independence at the United Nations. Sections three and four discuss the experiment with federalism and what the author terms 'governing democracy,' with section five presenting the liberal planning process and self-development. Section six enumerates the virtues of non-alignment.

Politics and Administration

230 **The nature of the reunification of Cameroon.**
Edwin Ardener. In: *African integration and disintegration.* Edited
by Arthur Hazlewood.   London, New York; Toronto: Oxford
University Press, 1967, p. 285-337. map.

Edwin Ardener is one of the most outstanding students of West Cameroo
(anglophone) society. In this essay he examines the process whereby the Englis
trust territory of Southern Cameroons became reunited with the French trus
territory of Cameroon to form the Federal Republic of Cameroon. Then follow
an analysis of the economic and political consequences of the reunification of th
two territories. Herein is presented a rare description of the state government c
West Cameroon. Quite accurately, Ardener suggests that the federation migh
end as a 'more centralized republic.' This took place in 1972 after a nationa
referendum.

231 **Aristocrats facing change: the Fulbe in Guinea, Nigeria, and
Cameroon.**
Victor Azarya.   Chicago; London: University of Chicago Press,
1978. 293p. map. bibliog.

The Fulbe or Fulani are a major population group in Northern Cameroon and i
several other African countries. In Cameroon they are a conquest group tha
came to dominate much of the North prior to the German conquest of the area
Azarya attempts here to utilize a comparative method of research to examine th
effects of colonial rule and independent governments on this Fulbe domination i
economic, political, and religious systems. He attempts to apply sociological too
to the study of history. His work is important not only as history, but as an aid t
our understanding of Cameroon politics, for the Fulbe remain an important grou
in the North and in the central government. Many observers, and man
Cameroonians, have assumed that Ahidjo (a Fulbe) was the front man for a Fulb
domination of the entire country. A shorter version of this book appearec
Dominance and change in North Cameroon: the Fulbe aristocracy (Beverly Hills
California; London: Sage, 1976).

232 **Ahmadou Ahidjo pionnier de l'Afrique moderne.** (Ahmadou
Ahidjo, pioneer of modern Africa.)
Beat Christophe Baeschlin-Raspail.   Monte-Carlo, Monaco:
Editions Paul Bory, 1968. 119p.

This tribute to former president Ahmadou Ahidjo as the 'pioneer' of moder
Africa is written in journalistic fashion. The first half of the book describes th
'twilight of colonialism,' while the second half concentrates on the rise an
consolidation of Ahidjo within what is entitled the 'Ahidjo era.' The Swiss auth
of this volume worked for two years as a journalist in Cameroon.

233 **La fonction politique des églises au Cameroun.** (The political
function of churches in Cameroon.)
Jean-François Bayart.   *Revue Française de Science Politique*, vol.
23, no. 2 (June 1973), p. 514-36.

The author describes the political aspects and roles of churches in Cameroon. H

76

begins with an examination of the relations of Cameroon's churches with the government, and goes on to denote the specific political functions of the churches. Churches, which are described as 'states within a state,' are subsequently viewed in terms of their contribution to political development in Cameroon.

234 **Clientelism, elections and systems of inequality and domination in Cameroun.**
Jean-François Bayart. In: *Elections without choice*. Edited by Guy Hermet, Richard Rose, Alain Rouquie. New York: John Wiley & Sons, 1978, p. 66-87.

Clientelism, or the existence of extensive networks of patron-client relationships, is common in most African states. Scholars argue that this is a cultural transfer from pre-colonial social and political systems. Bayart argues that this is true only in a limited sense and that such systems 'can be understood only in relation to the historical evolution of the structure of systems of inequality and domination' (p. 67) in African societies. He argues that the electoral process even in the Cameroon one-party system has played an important role in this historical evolution and that the elections are arenas of social struggle.

235 **L'Etat au Cameroon.** (The state in Cameroon.)
Jean-François Bayart. Paris: Presses de la Fondation Nationale des Sciences Politiques, 1979. 198p. bibliog.

This is an excellent discussion of the development of political structures and processes in Cameroon in the light of what the author terms a 'crise hegemonique.' An analysis is made of the accession to power of Ahmadou Ahidjo, the 'difficult years' of fighting the UPC (1958-1960), the consolidation of political power (1960-1962), and the continued rise of the single party state (1962-1976). Utilizing a more specific framework, Bayart discusses the transcendence of the clientel state, the positions of power within the Cameroon political structure, and the younger social groups attempting to carve out a new sphere of influence within the Ahidjo régime. Some of this material appears in the English translations of Bayart's essays.

236 **Cameroun: la révolution pacifique du 20 mai.** (Cameroon: the peaceful revolution of 20 May.)
Eno Belinga. Yaoundé: Lamaro, 1976. 198p.

The 'revolution pacifique' of May 20, 1972 refers to the date on which Cameroon became the 'United Republic' as opposed to its previous title of 'Federal Republic.' This essay exalts the unification process and the role of its leader, Ahmadou Ahidjo. The book examines the topics of 'people,' 'nation,' and 'fatherland.' Unification and the cultivation of youth within the nation are seen as the primary goals of the Cameroon nation. Extensive appendixes provide full length speeches by former President Ahidjo concerning topics such as the Cameroonian people, the unitary state and the Green Revolution.

Politics and Administration

237 **Les Camerounais occidentaux: la minorité dans un état bicommunautaire.** (The Western Cameroonians: the minority in a two-community state.)
Jacques Benjamin, preface by Jean Meynaud. Montréal: Les Presses de l'Université de Montréal, 1972. 250p. 2 maps. bibliog.

This examination of the salience and future success of the use of 'federalism' in bicultural societies in the furthering of political unification is based on a case study of Cameroon. The author discusses the effects of federalism on the minority anglophone group found in West Cameroon. The first half of the volume describes the effects that federal institutions have had on the political, economic, and administrative activities of West Cameroon. The second half describes how the dominant 'political culture' of French Cameroon has influenced the philosophy, language, and intercommunity relations of West Cameroon. Benjamin, a Canadian, develops a theory which is not specific only to the case study of Cameroon, but which can be applied generally, for example, to the case study of present-day Canada. The study is the result of the author's doctoral dissertation.

238 **Main basse sur le Cameroun: autopsie d'une décolonisation.** (Heavy hand on Cameroon: autopsy of decolonization.)
Mongo Beti, preface by Jacques Benjamin. Quebec, Canada: Editions Québécoises, 1974. 217p; Paris: François Maspero, 1977. 270p.

This scathing attack on the 'neo-colonialist' path of development followed in Cameroon and its subsequent 'plunder,' was censored by the Cameroon authorities. Beti denounces the rule of President Ahmadou Ahidjo and the 'odieuse machination' of the Cameroon National Union. An exploration is also made of the circumstances surrounding the capture, trial, and sentencing of Ernest Ouandie (former leader of the UPC) and Monseigneur Albert Ndongmo, a Catholic bishop convicted of aiding the UPC. The Paris edition contains a lengthy update by Beti.

239 **Cameroun: complots et bruits de bottes.** (Cameroon: conspiracies and the echo of boots.)
J.-P. Biyiti bi Essam. Paris: L'Harmattan, 1984. 117p. map.

The author, a Cameroonian and a former journalist, documents the events leading up to the attempted coup on April 6 and 7, 1984 by former President Ahmadou Ahidjo. Writing in journalistic fashion two weeks after the attempted coup, the study analyses Paul Biya's smooth succession to the presidency of Cameroon on November 4, 1982 and the subsequent growing Biya/Ahidjo hostility and political jockeying for influence. Useful annexes provide documents and statements which are relevant to the attempted coup, such as the full text of a radio message broadcast by the 'putschistes' on April 6, 1984.

240   **L'Administration Camerounaise.** (Cameroon administration.)
Alain Bockel.   Paris: Editions Berger-Levrault, 1971. 62p.
(Encyclopédie Administrative).

This is one of a general series devoted to the study of African administration within individual African nations. This volume centres on the topic of Cameroon administrative structures and procedures, and also discusses the legal basis of public administration in Cameroon. An appendix reproduces the law of June 14, 1969 which outlines the creation and parameters of the Federal Court of Justice and the decree of February 3, 1966 (modified on June 10, 1968) which is the 'General Statute of the Federal Public Function'.

241   **1st national council of the Cameroon National Union UNC.**
Cameroon National Union.   Yaoundé: CNU, 1967. 229p.

A collection of the major documents, speeches, and other important aspects of the first national council of the Cameroon National Union (CNU) held at Yaoundé, November 5-8, 1967. The book comprises the 'Programme of the National Council,' a list of CNU members present, the opening and closing addresses by President Ahidjo, and various statements by other members of the party. Topics discussed include the general role of the political party, relations between the party-government and the administration, the militant and the elections, the party's role in the implementation of the plan, party meetings, financial problems, and reports and resolutions.

242   **First Cameroon National Union Congress held in Garoua.**
Cameroon National Union.   La Loupe, France: SIPE, 1974. 303p.

The Cameroon National Union or the Union National Camerounaise (CNU or UNC) was the only political party in Cameroon. The reports of the three congresses held in 1969, 1975, and 1980 are important statements and indications of policy directions. Ahidjo's lengthy addresses to these congresses are the most important of the various speeches, though the sectional and special reports are also valuable. The lists of delegates serve as one indicator of membership in the Cameroon political élite. The congress reports are available in French and English versions. Also see A. Ahidjo's *Nation and development in unity and justice (q.v.)*.

243   **The Second Congress of the Cameroon National Union held in Douala, Cameroun.**
Cameroon National Union.   Yaoundé: CNU, 1975. 448p.

This is a collection of documents, speeches, and reports of the Second Congress of the Cameroon National Union (CNU) which was held between February 10 and 15, 1975. Among the various documents collected are messages from friendly political parties of other nations, financial receipts and expenditures of the CNU, a listing of important members within the political hierarchy of the party, and divisional section reports. These Congress reports are an important source of information on government policy.

244 **Ahmadou Ahidjo from A to Z: CNU 10th anniversary.**
Cameroon National Union. Yaoundé: CNU, 1976. 190p.

This pocket-sized collection of short quotes by Ahmadou Ahidjo on topics ranging from administration to the role of zeal in Cameroon today contains both French and English texts. The pamphlet exhaults the 'original experience' of Cameroon as the 'first bilingual African State.' It is a useful source of quotations on the policies of the Ahidjo years.

245 **L'UNC dans la nation: CNU in the nation.**
Cameroon National Union. Douala, Cameroon: CNU, 1980.
126p. bibliog.

The ideology of the Cameroon National Union is presented in this volume. The primary purpose of the document is to 'make available to the public a new publication for information and reflexion' and to answer the question 'What is the place and role of the Cameroon National Union within Cameroon?' A presentation of the history, facts, and doctrinal principles of the CNU is followed by general and specific prescriptions for practical action by the Party. Various realms of practical action include economic, cultural and social development, the inclusion of women and youth within the overall development framework, the nurturing of a 'sense of responsibility' or 'professional conscience,' and the role of party militants as a guarantee for the strengthening of institutions. The text is written in both English and French.

246 **L'Unité: actes de troisième congrès ordinaire de l'UNC de Bafoussam.** (Unity: Acts of the Third Ordinary Congress of the UNC at Bafoussam.)
Cameroon National Union. Yaoundé: CNU 1981. 255p.

As with the previous CNU congresses, the report of the Third Congress is a useful source of information on government policies and on those who are influential in Cameroon. As a result of the close intertwining of party and government in Cameroon, party documents have an official significance which is far greater than in many countries. Ahidjo's speech is thirty-four pages long.

247 **Paul Biya: le président de tous les Camerounais.** (Paul Biya: the president of all Cameroonians.)
Cameroon National Union. Yaoundé: CNU, 1985. 101p.

This booklet commemorates the Fourth Ordinary Congress of the Cameroon National Union held in 1985 in Bamenda under the leadership of President Paul Biya. The first section presents a brief biographical sketch of Biya, and the second section outlines his political philosophy, including the 'ethical foundations' of his 'renewal politics,' his attachment to 'national sovereignty,' and social thought. The final section examines Biya's programme of national integration and 'renewal contract.'

248   **As told by Ahmadou Ahidjo.**
Cameroon National Union, Political Bureau.   Monte Carlo,
Monaco: Paul Bory, 1968. 102p.

This collection of President Ahmadou Ahidjo's speeches commemorate the ten
years that he had spent attempting 'to create a Nation and ensure its development
amidst peace and justice, but also and perhaps above all to bear witness to his
vocation in the theological sense.' A brief biography of Ahidjo is followed by
short excerpts of past speeches pertaining to twenty-eight separate issues. The
four major groups of speeches revolve around the issues of political, economic,
social-cultural, and external political action.

249   **The political philosophy of Ahmadou Ahidjo.**
Cameroon National Union, Political Bureau.   Monte Carlo,
Monaco: Paul Bory, 1968. 121p.

This volume was designed as a tribute to the accomplishments of Ahidjo between
the years 1958 and 1968. It is also an attempt to synthesize the thoughts of Ahidjo
and transform them into a viable political philosophy which could act as a guide
for the citizens of Cameroon to follow. The fundamental themes of the book are
'Conception of the nation,' 'Conception of the state,' 'Views on development,'
and 'Humanism.'

250   **L'Oeuvre de la France au Cameroun.** (The work of France in
Cameroon.)
Pierre Chauleur.   Yaoundé: Imprimerie du Gouvernment, 1936.
258p. 10 maps.

The positive aspects of French colonial administration in Cameroon are
documented in this study. The author examines France's contribution to
agricultural and commercial development and the socio-political benefits of
providing medical personnel, school teachers, and religious missions. Infrastructural benefits, such as communication links, transportation networks, and
educational facilities, are also included. Extensive appendixes provide information on specific projects, accomplishments, and political groupings in various
regions and villages. The author was Administrator of Colonies and this work
relies heavily on official reports and documents.

251   **Territoires Africains sous mandat de la France: Cameroun et Togo.**
(African territories under the mandate of France: Cameroon and
Togo.)
Victor Chazelas.   Paris: Société d'Editions, 1931. 240p.

This examination of France's role as the administrator of the mandated territories
of Cameroon and Togo under the auspices of the League of Nations' Mandates
System, which was changed to the Trusteeship System under the United Nations,
was written by a former chief administrator of French colonies in Africa. It
presents the colonial argument, which emphasizes the positive effects of
continued French control through legal international means. Part one of the
volume provides a study of the French mandate concerning Togo and Cameroon.
An examination is made of the indigenous peoples, the German occupation, and

the Anglo-French partition of both nations. Part two discusses actual French administration of the territories. The emphasis here is on public services such as police forces, schools, and the postal networks provided by France.

252 **Native administration in the West Central Cameroons 1902-1954.**
Elizabeth Chilver. In: *Essays in imperial government*. Edited by
Kenneth Robinson, Frederick Madden. Oxford, England:
Blackwell, 1963, p. 91-139. 2 maps.

In 1902 a German imperial military station was built in Bamenda and in 1954 the Southern Cameroons received its first period of local political autonomy. This article describes the work of German and British political officers between these two dates in what the author calls West Central Cameroon. In addition, a description is made of the 'cross-current of Christianity' and the implementation of administrative decentralization and its limitations.

253 **L'Effort Français au Cameroun: le mandat Français et la
réorganisation des territoires du Cameroun.** (The French effort in
Cameroon: the French mandate and the reorganization of the
territories of Cameroon.)
René Costedoat, preface by Georges Scelle. Besançon, France:
Imprimerie Jacques et Demontrond, 1930. 288p. 4 maps. bibliog.

This work epitomizes the rationale utilized by the French to justify colonial rule in Cameroon. Costedoat defends the 'effort Français' by claiming that the nations colonized by the French were 'territories peopled by races incapable of evolving without the assistance of a nation qualified by its colonizing genius.' The mandates system is described as necessary and proper as well as a mutually beneficial arrangement through which Cameroon would develop as a territory under the auspices of French administration. Citations are made of France's commitment and contribution to social, economic, and political development in Cameroon. An extensive annex provides the reader with sixteen documents pertaining to French colonial rule. These consist mainly of extracts from annual colonial reports on social conditions.

254 **Cameroon: irrésistible ascension de M. Biya.** (Cameroon: the
irresistible rise of Mr. Biya.)
Philippe Decraene. *L'Afrique et L'Asie Modernes*, no. 138
(Autumn 1983), p. 3-11.

Decraene is one of France's most astute students of African affairs.

255 **United Republic of Cameroon.**
Mark W. DeLancey. In: *World encyclopedia of political systems
and parties*, vol. 1. Edited by G. Delury. New York: Facts on
File, 1983, p. 138-42. bibliog.

This brief overview of the Cameroon political process and its history is a useful introduction.

56 **Freedom and authority in French West Africa.**
Robert Delavignette. London: Cass, 1968. 152p.

This work, originally published in Paris as *Service Africaine* in 1946, presents the classic case for French colonial administration in Africa. Among other duties, the author was High Commissioner for the French Cameroons.

57 **Vers le mont Cameroun.** (Toward Mount Cameroon.)
Joseph Charles Doumba. Paris: Afrique Biblio Club, 1982. 187p.

This is an account of diverse discussions held between Joseph Charles Doumba and Jean-Pierre Fogin, two prominent Cameroonian scholars. They discuss the results of Cameroon's first three decades of independence (political, cultural, and socio-economic) in order to determine whether or not the fundamental options of Cameroon are the most appropriate in the socio-historical context of the countries of Africa and the Third World. The title signifies 'the march of the people towards their place of historical accomplishment,' or the success of the political, economic, and cultural development of Cameroon.

58 **Tentative de coup d'état au Cameroun: une réaction féodale.** (*Coup d'état* attempt in Cameroon: a feudal reaction.)
Daniel Ewandé. *Temps Modernes* (June 1984), p. 2,289-99.

A brief summary and analysis of former President Ahidjo's alleged attempt to seize power in 1984.

59 **Introduction à la politique Camerounaise.** (Introduction to Cameroon politics.)
Abel Eyinga. Paris: Editions Anthropos, 1978. 356p.

Writing in a revisionist fashion, the author presents Cameroon's political development as being essentially neo-colonialist in nature. The first two chapters describe the rise of nationalistic demands after the First World War and the suppression of these demands by the French colonial power in 1955. This is primarily shown by the French exclusion of the UPC from power and its ultimate suppression. Chapters three and four examine the institutionalization of the neocolonial political structure between 1956 and 1958, centering especially on United Nations intervention before the accession to independence of French Cameroon. Chapter five documents present day neocolonialism in Cameroon, with special emphasis on the growing necessity of government repression to maintain power.

60 **Mandat d'arrêt pour cause d'élections de la démocratie au Cameroun, 1970-1978.** (Arrest warrant for running in Cameroon's democratic elections, 1970-1978.)
Abel Eyinga. Paris: Editions l'Harmattan, 1978. 251p.

Abel Eyinga presents a personal account of his attempt to run for the presidency of Cameroon in the elections of 1970. Rather than being allowed to pursue his ambition, Eyinga was denounced by the ruling Cameroon government as a 'subversive' and therefore unable to present himself as a candidate, was extradited from a very cooperative France, and was finally sentenced to prison for five years by a military tribunal in Yaoundé. Eyinga denounces the ruling élite of Cameroon in general and the then President Ahidjo in particular, for not representing the true nationalist desires of the Cameroon people, but rather cementing a new colonialist relationship with France. The closed nature of Cameroon's supposedly 'democratic' elections is presented as evidence to support this claim. Eyinga describes the effects of this neo-colonialist relationship and Ahidjo's seemingly permanent state of emergency, eight years after the 197 elections, in terms of Cameroon's economy, foreign policy, sports, culture and education and health services.

261   **The one and indivisible Cameroon: political integration and socio-economic development in a fragmented society.**
John W. Forje, foreword by Jimoh Omo-Fadaka. Lund,
Sweden: University of Lund, 1981. 191p. map. bibliog.
The author presents a study of Cameroon integration focusing on the interplay between political integration, system change/social change, and political stability These three processes are viewed in terms of the manipulation and application of authoritarian, consensual, paternal, and identific variables. Three distinct period are examined: the era of federalism (1960-1966); the transition to unitar government and a single party within a federal context (1966-1972); and the period of time following the establishment of a unitary government (1972-1980) This is an excellent synthesis of traditional integration theory applied to a African nation. The study provides valuable lessons for African states in the process of 'nation-building' or attempting to forge a common identity for their peoples.

262   **Rapport annuel du gouvernement Français aux nations unies sur l'administration du Cameroun place sous la tutelle de la France.**
(Annual report of the French government to the United Nations on the administration of Cameroon placed under the trusteeship o France.)
French Government. Paris: Imprimerie National, 1947-. annual.
In conformity with Article 88 of the Charter of the United Nations, the coloni power governing a trusteeship territory must submit an annual report to the Secretary General concerning the administration of that territory. Similar report were issued annually to the League of Nations. Titles vary from year to year These are valuable documents, though the reader must remain aware that coloni administrators wished to paint a rosy picture of conditions and progress.

263   **Village communities and the state: changing relations among the Maka of Southeastern Cameroon since the colonial conquest.**
Peter Geschiere, translated by James J. Ravell. London; Boston, Melbourne: Kegan Paul International, 1982. 512p. 10 maps. bibliog.
The Maka, a Bantu-speaking people of South Eastern Cameroon, have not bee intensively studied by scholars. This important work examines the effects o German and French colonizaton on authority and government in Maka society

he author argues that colonialism imposed a strongly authoritarian structure on
he egalitarian system of the Maka, leaving the Maka today in an uneasy balance
etween the two. The implications for relations between Maka society and the
dependent government of Cameroon are considered. Important appendixes on
thnography, demography, local economics, and administrative organization
nder the French and current governments are included.

64 **Segmentary societies and the authority of the state: problems in
implementing rural development in the Maka villages of South-
Eastern Cameroon.**
Peter Geschiere. *Sociologia Ruralis*, vol. 24, no. 1 (1984), p. 10-
29.
he author claims that although African nations purport to have totalitarian
ureaucratic control over peasant societies, the reality is that the peasants remain
nincorporated by modern political-economic relations. This factor, along with
he articulation of capitalist and pre-capitalist relations and the autistic tendencies
f a national bureaucracy, are shown to retard rural development. The case study
hosen is the establishment of a rural cooperative in a Maka Village in South
astern Cameroon through a government programme entitled 'Zone d'actions
rioritaires intégrés' (Zone of integrated priority actions) (ZAPI).

65 **The Cameroon federation: political integration in a fragmentary
society.**
Willard R. Johnson.   Princeton, New Jersey: Princeton University
Press, 1970. 426p. map. bibliog.
his study, which is a landmark in its field applies integration theory to describe
he processes which, at the time, appeared to have made a success of the bilingual
olitical federation of Cameroon. Johnson 'shows how the 1961 federation of the
British and French Cameroons attempted to integrate a highly fragmented society
epresenting every social cleavage found in Africa, including disparate and
ilingual colonial legacies.' The first section outlines the theoretical basis of the
tudy, while section two delineates the historical background of the case study of
he Cameroon federation. The third section portrays the substance and extent of
he integrative advances in Cameroon.

66 **Gaullist Africa: Cameroon under Ahmadou Ahidjo.**
Edited by Richard Joseph.   Enugu, Nigeria: Fourth Dimension
Publishing Co., 1978. 217p.
Chapters by J. F. Bayart, Mongo Beti, Abel Eyinga, Philippe Lippens, Reginald
Green, and Richard Joseph examine the autocratic regime of Ahidjo and his
eocolonial dependence on France. Franco-Cameroonian relations, Cameroon's
omestic political system, the use of torture and the denial of human rights to
maintain that system, and the Cameroon economy are the major topics. This
olume stands as the most important attack on the Ahidjo regime in English.

Politics and Administration

267 **The impact of environment on ethnic group values in Cameroon.**
Ndiva Kofele-Kale. In: *Values, identities and national integration.*
Edited by J. N. Paden. Evanston, Illinois: Northwestern
University Press, 1980, p. 121-50.

This is an empirical investigation of the relationship between 'environmenta
locations' and 'ethnic group values' in anglophone Cameroon. The two majo
hypotheses examined are 'that ethnic ties and loyalty do not detract from nationa
orientations' and 'that variations in national political identification reflec
differences in environmental conditioning.' Two sets of data are employed to
determine variations in national political culture: environmental location (rura
villages, plantation camps, and large towns) and sense of ethnic grou
identification (membership consciousness, pride and group preservation throug
procreation and socialization).

268 **The impact of environment on national political culture in
Cameroon.**
Ndiva Kofele-Kale. In: *Values, identities and national integration.*
Edited by J. N. Paden. Evanston, Illinois: Northwestern
University Press, 1980, p. 151-72.

An examination is made of the relationship between environmental location an
national political orientations in Cameroon. More specifically, the article attempt
to determine if there is a significant difference of 'Political culture values' betwee
rural village, labour camp, and town residents in Cameroon. The author employ
and analyses extensive survey research data pertaining to media exposure an
four political culture subsystems: identity, symbol, rule, and belief.

269 **Tribesmen and patriots: political culture in a poly-ethnic African
state.**
Ndiva Kofele-Kale. Washington, DC: University Press of
America, 1981. 359p. map. bibliog.

This anglophone Cameroon author presents in this volume the results of hi
doctoral research conducted in Cameroon. Survey research and other technique
were used in this study of compatability between ethnic and national loyaltie
The author takes issue with Ahidjo's policies of nation-building, arguing tha
these policies increase ethnocentrism, rather than building a Cameroon nation
Kofele-Kale also argues that these two loyalties are not incompatible, and tha
African governments should not attempt to eliminate ethnic loyalties.

270 **Ethnicity, regionalism and political power: a post-mortem of
Ahidjo's Cameroon.**
Ndiva Kofele-Kale. In: *The political economy of Cameroon.* Editec
by Michael G. Schatzberg, I. William Zartman. Baltimore,
Maryland: Johns Hopkins University Press, 1986, p. 53-82.

The author, a political scientist from the anglophone portion of Cameroon
analyses the major sources of political conflict in the country and the overal
effects of the Ahidjo régime on the significance of those factors.

271   **Le Cameroun.** (Cameroon.)
Henri Labouret.   Paris: Centre d'Etudes de Politique Etrangère,
1937. 259p. 2 maps.

The author provides a descriptive account of French Cameroon as it existed in the
1930s. Firstly, a portrait is made of the social and moral condition, justice, and
social organization of the indigenous peoples of Cameroon. Secondly, the
economy of the territory is examined *vis-à-vis* the positive aspects of European
colonial administration. Subjects discussed include the building of infrastructure
within the territory, European colonization, and the European population in
residence. More specific economic topics, such as the roles of mining, public
finances, commercial activities, and commerce and the formation of capital are
also discussed.

272   **The Cameroons from mandate to independence.**
Victor T. LeVine.   Berkeley, California; Los Angeles: University
of California Press, 1964. 329p. 8 maps. bibliog.

The author provides an analysis of the history of political development in
Cameroon from when it was a League of Nations mandated territory under the
auspices of French rule to its independence as the Cameroon Republic. While the
major emphasis of the study is on the political development of French Cameroon,
the role and political development of British Cameroon is also described. Topics
elucidated include the pre-Second World War historical context and political
institutional growth, the ferment of party politics between 1945 and 1955, the
politics of consolidation (1955-1960), politics in British Cameroon, and the
problems of transition to an independent republic.

273   **The Cameroon Federal Republic.**
Victor T. LeVine, foreword by Gwendolen M. Carter.   Ithaca,
New York: Cornell University Press, 1971. 205p. 2 maps. bibliog.

The author examines the stability of the Cameroon Federal Republic since the
unification of the former British and French trusteeship territories in 1961. A
description of the historical background of Cameroon nationalism, independence,
and integration is followed by a portrait of its contemporary social setting and
political process. Contemporary issues discussed include national unity, economic
development, and external relations. Finally, LeVine puts into perspective
Cameroon's first decade of federation, noting its past problems and accomplishments and future prospects.

274   **Leadership and regime changes in perspective.**
Victor T. LeVine. In: *The political economy of Cameroon.* Edited
by Michael G. Schatzberg, I. William Zartman.   Baltimore,
Maryland: Johns Hopkins University Press, 1986, p. 20-52.

LeVine, one of the senior American students of Cameroon politics, discusses
Biya's recent succession to the presidency of Cameroon, the causes of the
succession, and the conflicts that followed the peaceful transfer of power. An
earlier article by LeVine, which is also useful is 'The politics of presidential
succession,' *Africa Report*, (May-June, 1983), p. 22-26.

Politics and Administration

275 **Rural local government in tropical Africa: examples from Tanzania and Cameroon.**
Philip Mawhood. *Cahiers Africains d'Administration Publique,* no. 6 (June 1971), p. 109-15.
The study compares and contrasts local government and administration in the rural areas of Tanzania and Cameroon. Specific topics discussed include areas of local government and its relationship with the central government, internal constitution, local finances, and local government functions.

276 **Les institutions politiques du Cameroun.** (The political institutions of Cameroon.)
Emile Mbarga. Yaoundé: Imprimerie Nationale, 1982. 210p. bibliog.
This is a concise text which illuminates the various processes and institutions that comprise the Cameroonian political system. The volume focuses on four key subject matters. Firstly, the system of voting and the role of referendums are described. Secondly, emphasis is placed upon the role of the strong presidency and its ministers. Thirdly, the power of the parliament and the links between it and the governing process are examined, and finally, an analysis is made of consultative and juridicial bodies such as, the Social and Economic Council and the High Court of Justice. An annex provides the reader with the constitution of the Cameroon Republic as adopted on May 20, 1972 and modified on May 9 and June 29, 1979. The volume is mainly descriptive.

277 **The political economy of development in Cameroon: relations between the state, indigenous business and foreign investors.**
Wilfred A. Ndongko. In: *The political economy of Cameroon.* Edited by Michael G. Schatzberg, I. William Zartman. Baltimore, Maryland: Johns Hopkins University Press, 1986, p. 83-110.
Although Cameroon follows a policy of capitalist development, the implementing of this policy leads to numerous conflicts between Cameroonian and foreign businessmen and investors. Government must regulate these conflicts, and, in doing so, often appears to favour foreign interests.

278 **Cameroun: qui gouverne? de Ahidjo à Biya, l'héritage et l'enjeu.**
(Cameroon: who governs? from Ahidjo to Biya, inheritance and stakes.)
Pierre Flambeau Ngayap. Paris: Editions L'Harmattan, 1983. 352p.
The purpose of this volume is to show the continuity and near absolute power embodied in the political system that was nurtured by Ahidjo and is now led by Biya through an examination of its inner workings and structures. The author portrays the hierarchy of influences and criteria for recruitment within the Cameroon government, the role and power of highly placed officials, civil servants, and the 'grands corps' (that is, ambassadors and the police), and the influence of powerful interests outside administrative circles. A discussion of the integration and resistance to change of the various groups of Cameroon's ruling class concludes the study.

79 **Traditional government and social change: a study of the political institutions among the Kom of the Cameroon Grassfields.**
Paul Nchoji Nkwi. Fribourg, Switzerland: Fribourg University Press, 1976. 233p. 3 maps. bibliog.

he author chose the Kom people of the Cameroon Grassfields as the focus of ▮is study because he is a citizen of the area. Nkwi describes social change among ▮e Kom in terms of the way in which political institutions evolved in the pre- and ▮st-colonial periods. The volume is divided into two parts: part one examines ▮aditional aspects of kingship, the administration of justice, and government at ▮c village level, with special emphasis being given to political associations; and ▮art two describes the process of change among Kom political institutions. The ▮lonial impact on traditional Kom political institutions is compared with the ▮st-colonial independent evolution of these same structures. Field research and a ▮rvey of published and archival material are the basis for this study, originally ▮e author's PhD dissertation.

80 **Cameroon grassfield chiefs and modern politics.**
Paul Nchoji Nkwi. *Paideuma*, no. 25 (1979), p. 99-115. bibliog.

he author examines the part played by the Southern Cameroons Grassfields ▮iefs in the political evolution of the region in the years preceding and following ▮ational independence. A description is provided of the power of pre-colonial ▮iefs, the initial arrangements preceding the creation of the 'House of Chiefs,' ▮e methods, motives, and choice of its members; and the essential elements of ▮e 1977 decree which reorganized the chiefdoms throughout Cameroon.

81 **Ethnic propensies for collaboration in Cameroon.**
Elone Nwabuzor. In: *Values, identities and national integration.*
Edited by J. N. Paden. Evanston, Illinois: Northwestern University Press, 1980, p. 231-58.

▮ata which elucidates the expressed propensies of the major ethnic groups in ▮ameroon to collaborate with one another are presented and evaluated. Both the ▮mension and patterns of interethnic collaboration are discussed. The various ▮thnic groups' propensies to collaborate are then correlated with 'ethnic value ▮stance.' Nwabuzor conducted survey research in anglophone Cameroon to ▮easure ethnocentrism.

82 **Ethnic value distance in Cameroon.**
Elone Nwabuzor. In: *Value, identities and national integration.*
Edited by J. N. Paden. Evanston, Illinois: Northwestern University Press, 1980, p. 205-29.

he author wishes to determine the patterns of similarities and differences ▮tween various ethnic groups in Cameroon with regard to group preferences for ▮rtain 'modal' and 'terminal' values. The success or failure of the politics of ▮ation-building 'may well depend on the commonality or incompatibility exhibited ▮y the several original political cultures.' Detailed descriptions are made of ▮ctoral differentiation and values, socialization and personal values, and ends ▮nd means values.

283 **Stability and instability in politics, the case of Nigeria and Cameroun.**
Nicholas D. Ofiaja, foreword by Claude E. Welch, Jr.   New York: Vantage Press, 1979. 223p. 5 maps. bibliog.

This adaptation of the author's doctoral dissertation compares the Nigerian an Cameroon political environments, finding them very similar, and compares thei political histories, finding them quite different. Cameroon is stable an progressing while Nigeria is not. According to Ofiaja, 'It is leadership roles an methods of conflict resolution with the elite cohesiveness that mark the differenc between the two nations.' (p. x).

284 **Dossier noir du pétrole Camerounais.** (Black dossier of Cameroon' petroleum.)
Organisation Camerounaise de Lutte pour la Démocratie (OCLD).   Paris: OCLD, 1982. 70p.

This booklet represents the viewpoint of the Cameroon Organization for th Struggle for Democracy (COSD) concerning the development of Cameroon i general and the use of its petroleum reserves in particular. The organizatio claims that Cameroon's petroleum reserves are being utilized for the benefit c foreign interests within a neocolonial framework rather than contributing to th basic development needs of the people of Cameroon. Furthermore, th organization claims that a kind of conspiracy exists in the upper echelons of th Cameroon government. The people of Cameroon are said to be deliberately kep in the dark and misguided as to the foreign businesses which exploit Cameroon' petroleum and with whom the UNC has contracts.

285 **Le Cameroun vers la lumière: manifeste de l'OCLD.** (Cameroon toward the light: manifesto of the OCLD.)
Organisation Camerounaise de Lutte pour la Démocratie (OCLD).   Paris: OCLD, [n.d.]. 101p.

The primary thesis and political stance of this manifesto of the Cameroo Organization for the Struggle for Democracy (COSD), as contained in th foreword is: 'Vingt ans de néo-colonialisme, ça suffit' (Twenty years of neocolonia ism, that's enough). The manifesto outlines the history of the Cameroo nationalist movement, the neocolonialist nature of Cameroon's politica economic, and cultural development, and the necessary political and economi guidelines for the true emancipation of the Cameroon people.

286 **Cameroun: an African federation.**
Neville Rubin.   London: Pall Mall; New York: Praeger, 1971. 259p. 3 maps. bibliog.

The author examines the historical processes that led to the federation of forme British and French Cameroon and the evolution of the policies and institutions o the new federal government. The first half of the book describes Cameroon' historical contacts with the Bornu and Fulani empires, as well as with Europea traders and colonialists. The specific aspects of German, French, and Britis colonial policies are set against Cameroon's political evolution under th international trusteeship and mandates systems. Also discussed are the rise of the UPC rebellion and the growth of an indigenous unification movement. The second half of the volume studies the specific aspects of Cameroon federalism, the results of reunification, unification and economic development, and Cameroon's position both in Africa and the world at large. An appendix provides the mandates and trusteeship agreements for French and British Cameroon.

287 Paul Biya and the quest for democracy in Cameroon.
Patrick Sam-Kubam, Richard Ngwa-Nyamboli, preface by François Sengat Kuo. Yaoundé: Editions CLE, 1985. 100p.
This study articulates and summarizes the changes that have taken place in Cameroon since the accession to power on November 6, 1982 of President Paul Biya. The volume is comprised of six chapters written by various Cameroon scholars. Richard Ngwa-Nyamboli in chapter one describes 'The story of a country lad who made it to the top.' Chapter two is a transcribed interview that Richard Ngwa-Nyamboli held with Professor Joseph Mboui who 'talks about Paul Biya as he knew him before he became President of Cameroon.' Chapters three and four by Patrick Sam-Kubam and Augustine J. Njawe discuss Paul Biya's 'political vision' and 'economic policy.' Peter Agbor-Tabi assesses Biya's role in contributing to social justice and Samuel Ekumu Fonderson summarizes Cameroon's new deal foreign policy.'

288 The metaphors of father and family.
Michael G. Schatzberg. In: *The political economy of Cameroon.* Edited by Michael G. Schatzberg, I. William Zartman.Baltimore, Maryland: Johns Hopkins University Press, 1986, p. 1-19.
This is an examination of the 'moral matrix' of the Cameroon political system.

289 Biya's new deal.
Frederick Scott. *Africa Report*, vol. 30, no. 4 (July-Aug. 1985), p. 58-61.
This article puts into perspective the 1985 Bamenda Party Congress convened by President Paul Biya and outlines the actions he must take to translate his newfound consensus into effective measures for change. Putting his troubled succession and the effects of the 1984 *coup* behind him, Biya has attempted to reorganize the party. This was signified by a change in the party name from the Cameroon National Union (CNU) to the Cameroon People's Democratic Movement (CPDM).

290 Recollections of British administration in the Cameroons and Northern Nigeria 1921-1957: 'But always as friends.'
Bryan Sharwood Smith. Durham, North Carolina: Duke University Press, 1969. 460p. 5 maps.
Writing in story form, the author traces the development of British colonial rule in Nigeria and the Cameroon. Smith's account is particularly revealing because he served in the British colonial service in Nigeria from the end of the First World War up to the granting of Nigerian self-government. The opening section of the

91

Politics and Administration

account, 'First as masters,' depicts the author's initial six years of work in Nigeria. Section two, 'Then as leaders' provides a detailed coverage of such topics as 'Sokoto in the twenties,' and 'Emir Usumanu of Gwandu,' and includes recollections of the Second World War. Section three entitled 'Finally as partners' describes the gradual handing on of power to native Nigerian leaders and institutions. During this period, parts of what is now Cameroon were attached to Nigeria and the author served as District Officer in British Cameroons. The volume was published in Great Britain as *But always as friends*.

291 **Persuasian and power in Cameroon.**
Frank M. Stark. *Canadian Journal of African Studies*, vol. 14, no. 2 (1980), p. 273-93.
The author analyses the relationships between persuasion, power, and authority in general, subsequently applying them to the case study of Cameroon.

292 **Urban unemployment as a determinant of political unrest: the case study of Douala, Cameroon.**
Joyce Sween, Remi Clignet. In: *Kamerun*. Edited by Hans F. Illy. Mainz, GFR: Hase and Koehler Verlag, 1974, p. 145-71.
The authors examine various hypotheses on the relationship between political unrest and urban unemployment. Data for the study is from a 1964 census of Douala. The conclusion reached is that each of the hypotheses has some validity.

293 **The one-party system and the African traditional institutions.**
Aletum Tabuwe. Yaoundé: the author, 1980. 63p. bibliog.
The purpose of this study is 'to point out the influences that traditional institutions have on the modern African one-party structure and the relationship between them.' The case study chosen is Cameroon. The author first traces the general development of African traditional systems and the modern African one-party structure, emphasizing the heterogeneity and 'life leadership' characteristic of African political systems and the roles of the military, traditional rule, and economic development. The author then provides a comparative analysis of the traditional and modern one-party system in Cameroon. The text is written in both English and French.

294 **Dream of unity: pan-Africanism and political unification in West Africa.**
Claude E. Welch, Jr. Ithaca, New York: Cornell University Press, 1966. 396p. 8 maps. bibliog.
Welch includes Togo, Cameroon, Senegambia, and the attempted union of Ghana, Guinea and Mali in this early but valuable study of African integration movements. The Cameroon section of about one hundred pages includes an excellent analysis of electoral politics in pre-independence anglophone Cameroon and the plebiscite conducted there in 1961. He shows the important interplay between the desire for independence and reunification and how this worked out differently in French and British Cameroons.

L'Année Politique et Économique Africaine. (The African Political and Economic Year.)
See item no. 1.

Area handbook for the United Republic of Cameroon.
See item no. 8.

Cameroon: United Nations challenge to French policy.
See item no. 100.

Cameroun Togo. (Cameroon Togo.)
See item no. 103.

Political evolution in the Cameroons.
See item no. 111.

Histoire des forces religieuses au Cameroon: de la première guerre mondiale à l'indépendence (1916-1955). (History of religious forces in Cameroon: from the First World War to independence (1916-1955).)
See item no. 130.

La république fédérale du Cameroun. (The Federal Republic of Cameroon.)
See item no. 302.

Le Cameroun: essai d'analyse économique et politique. (Cameroon: essay of economic and political analysis.)
See item no. 337.

A bibliography of Cameroon.
See item no. 500.

Law, Constitution and Land Tenure

295 **Islamic law in Africa.**
J. N. D. Anderson. London: Cass, 1970. 2nd ed. 409p.
Islamic law remains significant in most of northern and much of central
Cameroon. Although no extensive study of Islamic law in Cameroon is available,
this volume provides significant background material.

296 **Code du travail: labour code.**
Cameroon Government. Yaoundé: Government Printer, 1974.
165p.
The labour code sets the legal parameters for issues such as labour unions, work
contracts, salary, working conditions, and medical services. An index provides
quick access to particular technical and legal aspects of the code. Many such
publications are made available by the government on various aspects of the law.
As in this case, these are usually bilingual.

297 **Régime foncier et domanial: land tenure and state lands.**
Cameroon, Government Department of Lands. Yaoundé:
Government Printer, 1981. 152p.
These laws are particularly significant for the manner in which they provide for
the transfer of communal land to private ownership. The booklet is written in
both French and English.

298 **Limits to ritual resolution in Meta society.**
Richard G. Dillon. *Paideuma*, no. 25 (1979), p. 35-39.
In an effort to place Meta ritual resolution within a broader context of the Meta
system of law and conflict resolution, an analysis is made of whether all disputes
could adequately be resolved by this method, and if not, in which situations and
for what reasons did the Meta resort to alternative methods. Various cases

analysed which received non-ritual treatment in precolonial Meta society include theft, habitual witchcraft, adultery with the wife of a chief, flagrant defiance of village-level authorities, recovery of long-standing debts from members of other descent groups, and disputes over land and other property between members of different descent groups.

299 **Capital punishment in egalitarian society: the Meta' case.**
Richard G. Dillon. *Journal of Anthropological Research*, vol. 36, no. 4 (Winter 1980), p. 437-52.
The study of executions in egalitarian societies represents a neglected topic in the anthropology of law. The author, through a case study of the precolonial Meta society of the Cameroon highlands, fills this gap. Firstly, a presentation is made of the social and political organization and egalitarian nature of Meta society. This is followed by a discussion of coercive authority within Meta society and a description of life and death decision making as coordinated by the village chief. Finally, the sale of offenders as a self-help measure of Meta society is explained.

300 **Documentation législative Africaine.** (African legislative documentation.)
Dakar: Université de Dakar, Centre de Recherche, d'Etude et de Documentation sur les Institutions et les Législations Africaines, 1958-. annual.
Cameroon is one of the fifteen countries included in this listing of laws and decrees.

301 **Cameroon constitutional law: federalism in a mixed common-law and civil-law system.**
H. N. A. Enonchong. Yaoundé: Centre d'Edition et de Production de Manuels et d'Auxiliaires de l'Enseignement, 1967. 313p. bibliog.
The author, a Cameroonian, trained in law in England and the United States. This work is a revised version of his doctoral dissertation. In some respects it is now outdated, as the federation ended in 1972 and the constitution today is quite different from that of the 1960s when this book was written. However, the volume is important in analysing the historical development of the constitution, and Enonchong traces its roots through both British and French experience, though emphasis is on the British contribution. This volume is the best analysis in English of the federal constitution and is almost unique in its analysis of the bringing together in one system of British and French legal traditions. Sections on the central and state governments, human rights, the judiciary, and Cameroon nationality are included. Appendices contain the federal and both state constitutions.

302 **La république fédérale du Cameroun.** (The Federal Republic of Cameroon.)
P. F. Gonidec. Paris: Editions Berger-Levrault, 1969. 88p. map. bibliog. (Encyclopédie Politique et Constitutionnelle).
This volume is one of a general series devoted to the study of African constitutions and politics within individual African nations. Major sections cover political and constitutional evolution, political forces, 'present' political régime and the nature of society in Cameroon. An appendix provides constitutional documents which include the Constitution of the Federal Republic of Cameroon (September 1, 1961), that of East Cameroon within the Federal Republic (November 1, 1961), and that of West Cameroon within the Federal Republic (October 26, 1961). A second appendix provides the reader with primary texts and documents of the constitutions, federal institutions, and institutions of the federated states within the Cameroon Republic.

303 **Les institutions de droit public du pays Bamiléké (Cameroun): évolution et régime actuel.** (The evolution of public law in Bamileke Country (Cameroon): evolution and present regime.)
Enock Katté Kwayeb. Paris: R. Pichon, R. Durand-Auzias, 1960. 199p. 2 maps. bibliog.
The first half of the study is devoted to an explication of traditional Bamileke legal institutions. The sources and salient characteristics of traditional institutions are described. Political, judicial, and labour institutions are presented, as well as those which incorporate specific social or administrative functions. The second part of the book examines the modifications of traditional institutions because of practices and institutional frameworks brought from the metropolitan countries. Finally, a specific examination is made of the birth of urban and rural communes in the Bamileke regions, as a result of metropolitan influence.

304 **Legislation Camerounaise du travail.** (Cameroon labour law.)
E. Leunde. Yaoundé: CLE, 1983. 89p.
A summary and discussion of recent changes in Cameroon labour law.

305 **Eléments de droit bancaire Camerounais.** (Elements of Cameroon bank law.)
Ndjokou Mondjeli Mapeta. Yaoundé: the author, [n.d.]. 147p. bibliog.
This booklet enumerates the laws and regulations which are applicable to banking in Cameroon. Five chapters describe the essentials of commercial banks, finance establishments, control organs, the Bank of the Central African States, and public credit and savings institutions in Cameroon.

306 **La cour fédérale de justice du Cameroun.** (The Cameroon Federal Court of Justice.)
M. Nguini. *Recueil Penant*, no. 741 (July-Sept. 1973), p. 337-49.
The article examines the structure and process of Cameroon's Federal Court of

ustice as instituted on September 1, 1961. The author's comments place the
evolution of Cameroon's legal system in perspective as a description is also made
of the nation's new Supreme Court as enacted on June 2, 1972. The author's
arguments are capsulated at the end of the article in a philosophical manner, 'To
write law is nothing, to apply it well is everything.'

**607   Changes in land tenure and land use in a Bamileke chiefdom,
Cameroon, 1900-1980: an historical analysis of changes in control
over people.**
J. H. B. den Ouden. In: *Essays in rural sociology in honor of R. A.
J. van Lier.*   Wageningen, Netherlands: Agricultural University,
1981, p. 171-261.
Examines how land tenure and use allows governments to exercise control over
their people.

In French Cameroons, Bandjoon.
See item no. 37.

**Liste des thèses sur le droit Africain soutenues ou en préparation dans les
universités Françaises depuis 1974.** (List of theses on African law
completed or in preparation in French universities since 1974.)
See item no. 496.

Foreign Relations

308 **US bilateral assistance in Africa: the case of Cameroon.**
Peter Agbor-Tabi. Lanham, Maryland: University Press of
America, 1984. 180p. 2 maps. bibliog.

The thesis explored in this study is that 'adequate aid often does not reach the
intended beneficiaries due to institutional constraints in the donor and recipient of
aid.' The case study selected for examination is United States bilateral aid to
Cameroon through the Agency for International Development (AID). The author
highlights and proposes solutions to the specific problems that Cameroon has
experienced in maximizing the flow of aid to its stated targets. The book provides
an up-to-date account of individual USAID projects in Cameroon, empirical data
to elucidate who actually benefits from these projects and official USAID and
Cameroon Government responses as to why aid is misdirected. This case study,
which has practical application to all aid recipient nations, was originally the
author's PhD dissertation.

309 **In defense of peace, justice and solidarity in international society.**
Ahmadou Ahidjo. Yaoundé: [s.l.], ca. 1970. 74p.

The six speeches made by President Ahidjo before the Organization of African
Unity and the General Assembly of the United Nations are entitled 'Preserving
Africa's dignity,' 'Substituting the force of law,' 'Building a just and unified
world,' 'Placing science at the service of mankind,' '7th OAU Summit of the
Triumph of Unity,' and 'The United Nations Organization: the hope of mankind.'
The theme of the booklet is that these speeches 'constitute a veritable defence of
peace, justice and solidarity in International Society.'

310 **A political geography of Africa.**
E. A. Boateng. Cambridge, England: Cambridge University
Press, 1978. 292p. 34 maps.
This volume highlights the importance of boundary issues and conflicts over
territory in African international relations.

311 **African boundaries: a legal and diplomatic encyclopedia.**
Ian Brownlie. London: Hurst; Berkeley, California; Los
Angeles: University of California Press, 1979. 1,355p.
This is a standard reference on boundary questions in the study of African
international relations.

312 **Cameroon's foreign relations.**
Mark W. DeLancey. In: *The political economy of Cameroon.*
Edited by Michael G. Schatzberg, I. William Zartman.
Baltimore, Maryland: Johns Hopkins University Press, 1986,
p. 189-217.
Using a political economy approach, the author examines the effects of
Cameroon's colonial history as an influence on economic development and
foreign policies in the present period.

313 **The map of Africa by treaty.**
Edward Hertslet. London: HM Stationery Office, 1909, 3rd ed. 3
vols.
Important information on the origins of Cameroon's boundaries is provided in
this standard work on African boundaries in general.

314 **Cameroon and its foreign relations.**
Ndiva Kofele-Kale. *African Affairs*, vol. 80, no. 319 (April 1981),
p. 197-217. map.
Although foreign policymakers have denoted Cameroon's primary national
interests as the attainment of 'self-reliant development and national unity' as
guided by the principles of 'national independence,' 'nonalignment,' and 'regional
and international cooperation,' other factors have forced the government to
retreat from and adjust these principles. The primary reason for this retreat or
adjustment, as seen by Cameroon's policy of aligned nonalignment rather than
true non-alignment, is the nation's continued dependence on France. A
description is made of Cameroon's foreign relations with France and with other
major Western powers, with Israel and the Arab states of the Middle East, and
with 'sister' African states.

315 **The economic implication of multimembership in regional groupings: the case of Cameroon and Nigeria.**
Wilfred A. Ndongko. *Afrika Spectrum*, vol. 11, no. 3 (1976), p. 319-23.

The article describes and analyses the economic implications of Cameroon's and Nigeria's varying and dual memberships in regional economic groupings. While both nations are members of the Lake Chad Basin Commission (LCBC), Cameroon is a member of the Central African Customs and Economic Union (UDEAC) while Nigeria belongs to the Economic Community of West African States (ECOWAS). The possibility of some alternative trade arrangements in order to harmonize conflictual membership requirements are discussed.

316 **Le Cameroun dans les relations internationales.** (Cameroon in international relations.)
Adamou Ndam Njoya, preface by Charles Rousseau. Paris: R. Pichon et R. Durand-Auzias, 1976. 414p. 8 maps. bibliog.
(Bibliothèque Africaine et Malgache, vol. 26).

The author depicts the role and effects of international law on the political evolution of Cameroon. Firstly, an examination is made of the evolution of international law concerning various principalities. More specifically, Cameroon's place within international law before the First World War is described, including treaties signed between Cameroonians and the European colonial powers, those signed between the Europeans themselves, and the judicial nature of German rule. Secondly, Cameroon as an object of international law is portrayed. Included in this section is Cameroon as a mandated territory and subsequently as a trusteeship territory. Finally, the role of an independent Cameroon within the international legal system is analysed. The study is complemented by a 156 page annex which reprints 20 treaties, agreements, declarations, and accords issued by Cameroon, the colonial powers, and various international bodies.

317 **Introduction à la politique Africaine du Cameroun.** (Introduction to Cameroon's African policy.)
Dieudonné Oyono. *Le Mois en Afrique*, vol. 18, no. 207-8 (April-May 1983), p. 21-30.

Although Cameroon's major foreign policy efforts are with France, the Common Market, and the industrialized states of the West, the government has also made attempts to assume leadership in regional affairs with a focus on equatorial Africa.

318 **External influences and subimperialism in francophone West Africa.**
P-Kiven Tunteng. In: *The political economy of contemporary Africa*. Edited by P. C. W. Gutkind, I. Wallerstein. Beverly Hills, California: Sage, 1976, p. 212-31. bibliog.

This chapter centres on three key themes: the impact of France on the development of inequality in French West Africa; the rivalry between the major egional powers of Senegal and the Ivory Coast; and the impact that these factors will have on domestic justice and prospects for development in the region.

319 **Cameroon-Central African Republic boundary.**
US Department of State, Bureau of Intelligence and Research. Washington, DC: Department of State, 1970. 5p. map. bibliog. (International Boundary Study, no. 107).
Other documents in this series relevant to Cameroon are: *Cameroon-Nigeria boundary* (1969, no. 92); *Cameroon-Chad boundary* (1970, no. 102); *Cameroon-Congo (Brazzaville) boundary* (1971, no. 110); and, *Cameroon-Gabon boundary* 1971, no. 115).

Contribution to national construction.
See item no. 224.

Geographical Distribution of Financial Flows to Developing Countries.
See item no. 459.

African international relations: an annotated bibliography.
See item no. 486.

Nigeria and Cameroon: an annotated bibliography.
See item no. 493.

Economy and Economic Development

320 **L'Economie de l'ouest-Africain: perspectives de développement.**
(The economy of West Africa: perspectives on development.)
Osendé Afana. Paris: François Maspero, 1966. Reprinted 1977.
203p. bibliog. (Economie et Socialisme, no. 4).

An attempt is made to explicate the necessary conditions for fostering accelerated economic growth and development within individual nations of West Africa. Afana first presents a general overview of the dominant economic role of mono-crop export-based strategies of West African nations. The mono-crop emphasis on cocoa is the case study examined.

321 **Cameroon: an export market profile.**
Mary E. Burfisher. Washington, DC: US Department of
Agriculture, 1984. 32p. map. bibliog.

After a brief analysis of Cameroon's agricultural sector, the author discusses Cameroon's agricultural import needs and the potential for US exports to Cameroon.

322 **The Fifth Five-Year Economic, Social and Cultural Development Plan 1981-1986.**
Cameroon. Ministry of Economic Affairs and
Planning. Yaoundé: Ministry of Economic Affairs and Planning,
1981. 399p. 9 maps.

The Fifth Five-Year Development Plan (1981-1986) is the most comprehensive and detailed planning document drawn up by the Cameroon Ministry of Economic Affairs and Planning to date. The plan first outlines past economic growth and the structure and trends of external trade in Cameroon. An emphasis is placed on describing the fiscal aspects of financing the plan and determining growth prospects for the future. Specialized chapters describe the conditions

102

cessary for mobilizing female human resources, rural development, conditions cessary to dynamize administrative structures for development, and the growth ospects of the population. Other chapters are devoted to specific policies ncerning mining and industry, trade and transport, tourism, communications frastructures, youth and sport, and a host of other sectors. Especially formative and detailed is the section on education and training. Earlier plans, t referenced here, are valuable sources.

3 The summary of the Fifth Five Year Economic, Social and Cultural Development Plan.
Cameroon. Ministry of Economic Affairs and
Planning. Yaoundé: Ministry of Economic Affairs and Planniing, 1981. 100p.

brief examination of the economic trends in Cameroon during the Fourth evelopment Plan is followed by the basic methods of preparation, sectoral ogress reports and guidelines, and the growth and financing prospects of the fth Development Plan. Included is President Ahidjo's presentation address of e plan to the Cameroon National Assembly on November 4, 1981.

4 What you should know about the IIIrd. plan.
Cameroon. Ministry of Planning and Territorial
Development. Yaoundé: Ministry of Planning and Territorial Development, 1971. 72p.

his is a condensed version of Cameroon's Third Five Year Development Plan. ne booklet first summarizes demographic trends and economic growth since 64/1965. Secondly, basic policies, sectoral programmes, means of financing, and verall economic effects of implementation of the Third Development Plan are utlined. The introduction to the booklet contains various speeches made by inisters and by President Ahidjo marking the presentation of the plan to the ameroon National Assembly on August 11, 1971.

5 Cameroon special: the drive for development.
AfricaAsia, no. 12 (Dec. 1984), 54p.

his special edition on the Cameroon economy contains essays on politics, dustrial development, transportation, urbanization, education and foreign ade.

6 Cameroon survey.
African Business (London), vol. 12-(Dec. 1982), p. 47-72.

rticles include 'Ahidjo hands over the helm,' 'Successful dynamic duo: oil and ood management,' 'Moving into the oil age with discretion,' 'Unique level of ood self-sufficiency,' 'Agro-industry a key to national strategy,' 'Top funds armarked for roads and railways,' 'Potential is there to bridge power gap,' izing up future mineral wealth,' and 'New arrivals stiffen competition.'

327 **Le Cameroun.** (Cameroon.)
Marchés Nouveaux, no. 9 (1977), 91p.

This publication provides the businessman in particular and those interested Cameroon in general with an analysis of investment opportunities in the nation. brief summary of Cameroon is followed by an enumeration of the sociopolitic situation and the economic life of the nation. The primary emphasis of the serie however, is on succinctly classifying possibilities for export and investment a complementary networks of transport and communication. Two appendix provide the existing investment codes and interior production taxes, as well as extensive list of useful business addresses. Though now somewhat dated, th remains a useful account.

328 **Cameroon: les grands enjeux du renouveau.** (Cameroon: the great games of renewal.)
L'Afrique diplomatique, économique, financière, no. 2 (1985), 106p. 2 maps.

Brief essays on agriculture, mining and power, industry, the five-year pla foreign trade, politics, education, health, the press, music, and tourism a included along with numerous tables of data. Emphasis on most of the reports on the Biya years and a positive view of the future.

329 **Cameroun: une nouvelle étape.** (Cameroon: a new step.)
J. M.Clair (et al). *Europe Outremer*, vol. 59, no. 637-638 (1983) 52p. map.

An issue of this journal is prepared annually on Cameroon. Brief essays c agriculture, forestry, the development plan, and other aspects of the economy a included.

330 **L'Economie Camerounaise.** (The Cameroon economy.)
Bulletin de l'Afrique Noire. Paris: Ediafrica-La Documentation Africaine, 1979. 3rd ed. 238p.

This publication, which is a special edition of the *Bulletin de l'Afrique Noi (BAN)*, provides an extensive overview of the Cameroon economy. Combinir up-to-date statistics with concise analyses, the edition elucidates specific aspects Cameroon's economy such as finances, credits, telecommunications, agricultur urbanization, tourism, and industry. Especially interesting is a discussion of th implementation of the first two years of Cameroon's fourth development pla (1976-1981).

31 **Evolution des emplois et des ressources des banques commerciales du Cameroun au cours de l'exercise 1978-1979 et leurs résultats d'exploitation.** (The development of jobs and resources in commercial banking in Cameroon during the 1978-1979 financial year and their operational results.)
Banque des Etats de l'Afrique Centrale, Etudes et Statistiques (Yaoundé), no. 77, (Dec. 1980), p. 323-48.
Cameroon is a member of the franc zone and of the Bank of the States of Central Africa. Essays in this publication of the bank discuss monetary matters relating to Cameroon.

32 **The economy of Cameroon Federal Republic.**
R. H. Green. In: *The economies of Africa*. Edited by P. Robson, D. A. Lury. Evanston, Illinois: Northwestern University Press, 1969, p. 236-86. map. bibliog.
This general, descriptive survey of the Cameroon economy at the time of independence is guardedly positive about the economic future of the country. The discovery of petroleum some years after this essay was written would make the author even more positive. The most useful section of this paper discusses economic planning and development strategy. The author analyses French colonial strategies as well as those of the independent government. The discussion of human resources – health, nutrition, education, and the labour force – though brief is an important contribution. Emphasis in the discussion is on East or francophone Cameroon.

33 **Black Africa develops.**
William A. Hance. Waltham, Massachusetts: Crossroads Press, 1977. 158p. 9 maps.
This general introduction to the problems of economic development, written by a geographer, presents the orthodox view of most European and American scholars. It is written for the non-specialist.

34 **Analyse du sous-développement en Afrique Noire: l'exemple de l'économie du Cameroun.** (Analysis of underdevelopment in black Africa: the example of the Cameroon economy.)
Philippe Hugon, preface by André Philip. Paris: Presses Universitaires de France, 1968. 325p. 13 maps. bibliog.
The theme of this study is that underdevelopment has occurred in Cameroon because of the 'partial destruction' and 'survival' of its 'traditional equilibrium.' An examination is made of various factors which constrain economic growth, including sociocultural and institutional variables, the disarticulation of the economy, and economic dependence on external powers. Various factors which exemplify disequilibrium of growth, such as the demographic explosion, budgetary pressures, inflation, and unequal social stratification, are individually discussed. The author reviews Cameroon's efforts at national planning (1960-1970), and presents the basic orientations for and the potential of a new strategy.

335 **Kamerun: Strukturen und Probleme der sozio-ökonomischen Entwicklung.** (Cameroon: structures and problems of socio-economic development.)
Edited by Hans F. Illy. Mainz, GFR: Hase and Koehler Verlag, 1974. 348p. 2 maps. bibliog. (Institut für Internationale Solidaritat. no. 12).

Fifteen essays in German, French, and English by European, American, and one Cameroon scholar are included in this volume. Demography; economic development and planning; migration and urbanization; agriculture and cooperatives; and a well-developed bibliography are the major topics.

336 **Surveys of African economies.**
International Monetary Fund. Washington, DC: International Monetry Fund, 1968. vol. 1. 365p. 6 maps.

This volume examines the economies of the central African countries. In addition to the chapter on the Cameroon economy, there are important chapters on the Union Douanière et Economique de l'Afrique Centrale (UDEAC) and on several aspects of the economies of the member states. Banking, balance of payments and exchange and trade control are major topics. The Cameroon chapter although somewhat dated, presents a good general description of the economy. It includes sections on: development plans; prices, wages, and employment; finance money and banking; and foreign aid, trade, and investment. Twenty-nine tables provide data for the period 1960 to 1966.

337 **Le Cameroun: essai d'analyse économique et politique.** (Cameroon: essay of economic and political analysis.)
David Kom, preface by Jean Suret-Canale. Paris: Editions Sociales, 1971. 334p. 3 maps. bibliog.

Utilizing a Marxist-Leninist model, the author describes the political and economic neocolonialist development of Cameroon. Cameroon's remarkable agricultural and industrial growth is seen as not serving national interests, but rather those of the foreign monopolies in the industrialized countries. An analysis is made of the growth of classes and class struggle in Cameroon followed by a description of the structure and fundamental givens of the Cameroon economy. Cameroon's economy is subsequently examined in terms of its economic relations with the capitalist, African, and socialist nations. The conclusion is devoted to the explanation of an alternative or non-capitalist path of development which the author believes Cameroon should follow.

338 **A comparative analysis of French and British investment policies in Cameroon.**
Wilfred A. Ndongko. *Pan-African Journal*, vol. 7, no. 2 (Summer 1974), p. 101-10.

This analysis examines differential effects on the economies of former East Cameroon (a former French trust) and former West Cameroon (a former British trust). The author claims that an examination of the 'magnitude' of British and French aid to these two areas 'will broaden our understanding of the various sectoral shifts that occurred in the two economies prior to independence and reunification.' The net conclusion is that economic and social disparities between the two regions are due to differing French and British public and private sector policies.

339   **Planning for economic development in a federal state: the case of Cameroon, 1960-1971.**
Wilfred A. Ndongko.   Munich: Weltforum Verlag, 1975. 214p. bibliog.

'The purpose of this study is to develop a framework for examining the process of planning for economic development under federalism and to utilize the framework to examine the Cameroonian experience from 1960-1971.' (p. 11). The author, an outstanding anglophone Cameroon economist, argues, quite correctly, that economic development took precedence over federalism and that eventually West Cameroon would be assimilated by East Cameroon. This volume is a key source of data on the economy of anglophone West Cameroon.

340   **The external trade pattern of Cameroon, 1957-72.**
Wilfred A. Ndongko.   *Africa Quarterly*, vol. 16, no. 1 (July 1976), p. 76-87.

The article, although dated, provides a useful analysis and summary of Cameroon's trade, especially with France.

341   **The financing of economic development in Cameroon.**
Wilfred A. Ndongko.   *Africa Development*, vol. 2, no. 3 (1977), p. 59-76.

Cameroon has financed its development by seeking foreign public and private funds and by drawing on domestic resources, essentially restricting consumption through higher tax rates and efficiently utilizing idle national resources. The author examines financing in the 1960-65, 1966-71, 1971-76, and 1976-81 national development plans. Three features characterize development financing in Cameroon: diversification of sources of investment financing with an emphasis on domestic contributions; dominance of the state budget in the financing of public capital works; and reduction of investment funds allocated to the infrastuctural sector in favour of increased allocations to the industrial, mining, energy, and agricultural sectors.

342   **Un instrument quantitatif d'analyse macro-économique pour l'Afrique centrale: cas du Cameroun.** (A quantitative instrument for macroeconomic analysis in Central Africa: the case of Cameroon.)
Jean Nkuété, preface by Georges Ngango.   Yaoundé: Editions CLE, 1977. 81p. bibliog.

This work is an economist's attempt at determining the optimal rate of growth for underdeveloped economies in general and Cameroon in particular. The first half of the study is devoted to an analysis of various methods for the 'autonomous determination' of the universal global objective of growth. The second half, utilizing a vast repertoire of mathematical formulae and equations, presents an econometric model for the determination of secondary objectives inherent in the overall objective of growth, such as production.

343 **Monnaie et finances comme moteur de développement: le cas du Cameroun.** (Money and finances as the driving force of development: the case of Cameroon.)
Jean Nkuété. Yaoundé: Editions CLÉ, 1980. 262p.

The purpose of this volume is to describe the role that money and finance have played in fostering Cameroon's development. The first half of the book discusses money and finances before independence. Separate sections cover rivalry between the major powers (1472-1884), German colonization (1884-1918), and French and British colonization. The second half highlights the role of money and finances in the post-independence period.

344 **Regional policy in Cameroon: the case of planning without facts.**
Walter H. Rambousek. *Geoforum*, vol. 13, no. 2 (1982), p. 163-75.

The author argues that 'in spite of government rhetoric, no regional development policy (in Cameroon) as normally defined exists. What does exist are the regional effects of development projects.'

345 **Planification économique et projections spatiales au Cameroun.**
(Economic planning and spatial projections in Cameroon.)
Gabriel-Alexis Sobgui, preface by J. Marczewski. Paris: Nouvelles Editions Debresse, 1976. 255p. 13 maps. bibliog.

An in-depth discussion of the regional, national, and international spatial aspects of national planning in Cameroon is followed by an account of the conditions and demands of a genuine strategy for spatial projection of economic planning in Cameroon. Inclusive in this section are the specific material and technical conditions, constraints of an open economy, and demands of democratization within the over all planning process.

346 **The general report. The economic potential of West Cameroon, priorities for development. Vol. 1.**
Stanford Research Institute. Menlo Park, California: Stanford Research Institute, 1965. 98p. 3 maps.

This study of the West Cameroon economy was published in several volumes, all of which are reviewed in this volume. Other volumes are devoted to agriculture, public health, transport and telecommunications, tourism, industry, education and manpower, and finance.

347 **Etude comparée des politiques économiques du Cameroun et de la Côte d'Ivoire.** (Comparative study of the political economies of Cameroon and the Ivory Coast.)
Gilbert Tixier.   Paris: Librairie Générale de Droit et de Jurisprudence, 1973. 182p. 2 maps. bibliog.

In this comparative analysis of the political economies of Cameroon and the Ivory Coast, the history, geography, and key economic points of the two countries are first presented. Then, an examination is made of the fiscal and investment policies designed within the particular political framework of each nation. The extent of state interventionism and planning is discussed in terms of their dangers, positive aspects, and subsequent problems of development in the last section of the pamphlet.

348 **The practices of a liberal political economy: import and export substitution in Cameroon (1975-1981).**
Jean-Claude Willame. In: *The political economy of Cameroon.* Edited by Michael G. Schatzberg, I. William Zartman. Baltimore, Maryland: Johns Hopkins University Press, 1986, p. 111-32.

Export-substitution (the development of local industries to replace dependence on foreign sources of manufactured goods) has been a major aspect of Cameroon's economic development planning. The efficacy of that policy is examined in this article.

L'Année Politique et Économique Africaine. (The African Political and Economic Year.)
See item no. 1.

Cameroon: forward with confidence.
See item no. 2.

L'Encyclopédie de la République Unie du Cameroun. (Encyclopaedia of the United Republic of Cameroon.)
See item no. 3.

Area handbook for the United Republic of Cameroon.
See item no. 8.

Cameroun Togo. (Cameroon Togo.)
See item no. 103.

U.S. bilateral assistance in Africa: the case of Cameroon.
See item no. 308.

Tableaux économiques du Cameroun. (Cameroon economic tables.)
See item no. 458.

Economy and Economic Development

Bibliography of West Cameroon: economic development literature.
See item no. 479.

Women and economic development in Cameroon.
See item no. 481.

Industry, Transport and Communications

49 A suggested program for transport and telecommunications. The economic potential of West Cameroon, priorities for development, Vol. 4.
Phillip L. Adams, Frank L. Turner.   Menlo Park, California: Stanford Research Institute, 1965. 146p. 10 maps. bibliog.
Although this study was limited to anglophone Cameroon and it is now rather dated, it provides useful data on roads, ports, air transport, and tele-communications.

50 Strategic highways of Africa.
Guy Arnold, Ruth Weiss.   London: Julian Friedmann, 1977. 178.
maps.
Roads, railroads, and rivers are discussed in this volume.

51 Complexes agro-industriels au Cameroun. (Agro-industrial complexes in Cameroon.)
J. C. Barbier, G. Courade, J. Tissandier.   Paris: ORSTOM, 1980. 281p. 26 maps. bibliog. (Travaux et Documents de l'ORSTOM, no. 118).
These essays examine the contributions of complex agro-industries to the development of Cameroon. The first essay by G. Courade discusses Unilever, a multinational firm which at present cultivates 10,000 hectares of land and employs 3500 workers (the Plantations Pamol du Cameroun Limited) in one of the least developed zones in Cameroon. The second essay by J. C. Barbier and J. Tissandier explains the impact that the construction of a sugar refinery has had on the town of Mbandjok. The third essay by J. C. Barbier centres on the agro-industrial region of Obala-Nanga-Eboko. More specifically, a discussion is made of the specific agro-industries created and the social problems that they cause. All

three essays utilize a wealth of statistical data to emphasize their hypotheses a■ conclusions.

352 **The Cameroons Development Corporation: partner in national growth.**
Sanford H. Bederman, foreword by Victor Mukete. Bota, West Cameroon: Cameroons Development Corporation, 1968. 80p. 6 maps.

This work presents the historical development of the Cameroons Developme■ Corporation (CDC) from its origins in the German colonial plantations a■ discusses the role and contribution it has made to national development Cameroon. The author discusses the CDC's physical and historical backgroun■ organization and finance, labour, crops (bananas, oil palms, rubber, tea, coco■ and pepper), research, and transport and communications. Those interested the history of the plantations viewed from the broader perpective of Camero■ political and economic development should refer to Simon Joseph Epal■ *Plantations and developments in Western Cameroon, 1885-1975: a study agrarian capitalism* (New York: Vantage, 1985. 251p. 3 maps. bibliog.).

353 **The Cameroon Development Corporation, 1947-1977: Cameroonization and growth.**
Sanford H. Bederman, Mark W. DeLancey. In: *An African experiment in nation-building.* Edited by Ndiva Kofele-Kale. Boulder, Colorado: Westview Press, 1980, p. 251-78. 3 maps.

The authors present an historical sketch of this giant government-own■ plantation company. This is followed by a discussion of the financial a■ personnel factors that have been so critical to the Corporation's success since t■ independence of Cameroon.

354 **The Transcameroonian.**
John I. Clarke. *Geographical Magazine*, vol. 40, no. 15 (July 1968), p. 1,268-77. map.

The article is a brief presentation of Cameroon's transportation system in gener■ and the construction of the Transcameroonian Railway which began in Octob■ 1964. The railway, which was Cameroon's initial major project for linking t■ north and south regions of the nation, is described in terms of initial Germ■ railroad projects, 'grandiose' early schemes, competing road traffic, and extern■ outlets for the finished line.

355 **African trade unions.**
Ioan Davies. Harmondsworth, England: Penguin, 1966. 256p. bibliog.

Though now rather dated, this volume presents a useful general introduction the subject.

56 **Oil reserves and the Cameroonian economy.**
Shantayanan Devarajan, Nancy C. Benjamin. In: *The political economy of Cameroon.* Edited by Michael G. Schatzberg, I. William Zartman. Baltimore, Maryland: Johns Hopkins University Press, 1986, p. 161-88.
Oil and agriculture are Cameroon's main economic bases. Although the discovery and subsequent exploitation of the country's petroleum reserves are rather recent, oil has already had, and will continue to have, major effects on the Cameroon economy. Experience elsewhere has shown that those effects can be both positive and negative. The authors examine these effects and consider the possible future relationships between petroleum and the overall economy.

57 **The economic potential of West Cameroon – priorities for development: industry. Vol. 6.**
Peter D. Duncan. Menlo Park, California: Stanford Research Institute, 1965. 88p. 3 maps.
This volume of the report contains suggestions for courses of action for exploiting and realizing West Cameroon's industrial potential. Various sectors of the economy discussed include mining; oil and natural gas; electric power; environment and opportunities for the manufacturing and service industries; agricultural and animal products; textiles; forest and forest products industries; paper, printing, and publishing industries; chemical industries; metalworking industries; and leather, rubber and plastic, and ceramic industries. Cost implications of the industrial programme are discussed. Useful appendixes summarize import trends, investment codes, and other data (up to 1965) relevant to economic development in West Cameroon.

58 **Pilot study on social criteria for development cooperation.**
International Institute for Labour Studies, preface by Albert Tevodrijre. Geneva: International Labour Organisation, 1981. 163p. (International Institute for Labour Studies, Research Series no. 48).
The pilot study explores 'possiblities for giving greater attention to social concerns in the various stages of co-operation projects.' More specifically, an examination is made of how to promote productive socioeconomic integration of basic human needs satisfaction, employment, and participatory organization of target populations into the 'main stream' of development. The case study which is the core of the project is the Cameroon Development Corporation (CDC). The first part of the study provides the methodology utilized and background information on CDC operations in Cameroon. The second part presents the findings of the case study with the third offering general conclusions and recommendations.

59 **Plantation workers: conditions of work and standards of living.**
International Labour Office. Geneva: International Labour Office, 1966. 248p. bibliog. (Studies and Reports, New Series, no. 69).
This publication explores the living standards and working conditions of

plantation workers in twelve nations located in three continents: Afric (Cameroon, Ivory Coast, Mauritius, Tanganyika); Latin America (Colombia Costa Rica, Ecuador, Peru); and Asia (India, Indonesia, Malaya). First, a look i taken at the plantation labour force and the work they do *vis-à-vis* the nationa and international environments. Second, conditions of work and labou management relations are described in terms of wages, hours of work, status o women and young workers, workmen's compensation, social security, and labou inspection. Finally, standards of living are explicated through the factors o housing, food, clothing, education, hygiene and health, welfare facilities, an family budgets and purchasing power.

360   **Studies in industrialization: Nigeria and the Cameroons.**
      F. A. Wells, W. A. Warmington.   London: Oxford University
      Press, 1962. 266p. 2 maps.
The authors reveal the process of industrial development through an examination of individual industries and enterprises in Nigeria and West Cameroon. The analyse labour policies and working conditions, wage structures, absenteeism labour/management relations, industrial productivity, trade unions, and join consultation in order to explain the factors necessary for successful industrializa tion. Included in the overall analysis is a description of the societal and politica aspects of industrialization. The Cameroons Development Corporation is a majo case study.

Le Cameroun fédéral. (Federal Cameroon.)
See item no. 9.

French Equatorial Africa and Cameroons.
See item no. 142.

Le Cameroun. (Cameroon.)
See item no. 327.

L'Economie Camerounaise. (The Cameroon economy.)
See item no. 330.

African trade unionism: a bibliography with a guide to trade union organizations and publications.
See item no. 495.

Agriculture and
Animal Husbandry

361 Agriculture d'exportation et bataille du développement en Afrique tropicale: l'économie du cacao. (Export agriculture and battle of development in tropical Africa: the cocoa economy.)
Jean Assoumou, preface by J. M. Albertini. Paris: Jean-Pierre Delarge, 1977. 351p. map. bibliog.

The growth and export of cocoa is a major agricultural business in West Africa. The author examines the chances of development for an African nation when the economy is dominated by a primary export product, in this case cocoa. The first half of the book centres around the general evolution and specific aspects of cocoa agriculture within the world economy. A detailed analysis is made of how world prices for cocoa are set and the inherent problems between producers and consumers of this product. The second half of the study is devoted to a case study of the cocoa industry in Cameroon. Specific topics discussed include Cameroon's large cocoa plantations, family production of cocoa and the commercialization of cocoa production in general. Finally, the role of cocoa production and export as a contributor to economic development in Cameroon is assessed.

362 The marketing of food crops in the Eastern Province of Cameroon.
E. A. Atayi, H. C. Knipsheer. *International Institute of Tropical Agriculture: Agricultural Economics Discussion Paper.* Ibadan, Nigeria: IITA, 1980, p. 1-27.

363 The demise of the commercial banana industry in West Cameroon.
Sanford H. Bederman. *Journal of Geography*, vol. 70, no. 4 (April 1971), p. 230-34. 3 maps.

Banana production became very important in the period 1947-1960, but by 1965 it had declined, due to disease, climate, and international trade factors. Concurrent with the rise in importance of banana production was the growth of an extensive cooperative structure, the Bakweri Co-operative Union of Farmers Ltd. (BCUF).

Agriculture and Animal Husbandry

364   **Quel développement rural pour l'Afrique noire?** (What rural
       development for black Africa?)
       Guy Belloncle.   Dakar, Abidjan: Les Nouvelles Editions
       Africaines, 1979. 209p.
This modern classic development theory examines the problems and prospects of
rural development in sub-Saharan Africa. The case studies chosen for examination are two separate regions of Cameroon (Centre/South and East) which are
government-targeted 'Priority zones for integrated action' (ZAPI). The author's
primary hypothesis is that the source of development problems within the rural
areas is not the individual African peasant, but rather the 'total inadequacy of
recommended development strategies and popularized methods practiced.'

365   **Agriculture in Cameroon.**
       Cameroon. Ministry of Information and Culture.   Yaoundé:
       Ministry of Information and Culture, 1975. 95p.
This pamphlet presents a concise overview of Cameroon agriculture. The first
chapter describes food crops (cereals, tubers, vegetables, oil seeds, and fruits)
which are grown in the nation. The second chapter emphasizes industrial and
export products, such as cocoa, coffee, cotton, bananas, oil palms, tea, tobacco,
spices, chinchona bark, and rubber, while chapter three discusses the livestock in
Cameroon, emphasizing the role of the state and perspectives for national
development.

366   **Cameroun, Congo, Gabon, Empire Centrafricain, Tchad: résultats
       du recensement agricole 1972/73 pour le Cameroun.** (Cameroon,
       Congo, Gabon, Central African Empire, Chad: results of the
       agricultural census 1972/1973 for Cameroon.)
       Rome: FAO; UNDP, 1977. 360p. 11 maps. (AG:
       DP/RAF/71/186).
Statistical tables, maps, tables and analysis of information on Cameroon
agriculture provide a dated, but historically useful base for the study of Cameroon
agriculture.

367   **Cameroon national food policies and organizations: the Green
       Revolution and structural proliferation.**
       Mark W. DeLancey.   *Journal of African Studies*, vol. 7, no. 2
       (Summer 1980), p. 109-22.
A brief description of the Cameroon Green Revolution indicates optimistic goals
and that many new institutions must be established to reach these goals. Evidence
is presented that it will be difficult to staff these institutions.

368 **Agricultural productivity in Cameroon.**
Virginia DeLancey. In: *The political economy of Cameroon.*
Edited by Michael G. Schatzberg, I. William Zartman.
Baltimore, Maryland: Johns Hopkins University Press, 1986,
p. 133-60.
Numerous factors influence agricultural productivity examined here, both in terms of production per unit of labour, and production per unit of land. Overall, productivity in Cameroon is very low. DeLancey examines the causes of this and suggests alterations in agricultural and rural development policies to increase productivity. DeLancey's general views on agricultural policy are presented in her essay 'Cameroon agricultural policy: the struggle to remain food self-sufficient', in *Dependency theory and the return of high politics*, edited by M. A. Tetreault and C. F. Abel, (Westport, Connecticut: Greenwood, 1986, p. 246-316.).

369 **Comportements socio-économiques en milieu de plantation Eton (Cameroun).** (Socio-economic behaviours in the Eton plantation environment (Cameroon).)
B. Delpech. *Cultures et Développement*, vol. 14, no. 4 (1982),
p. 639-79.
The author analyses the way in which the importation and institutionalization of cocoa farming has upset the conditions of life and transformed the mentalities of the people living in Southern Cameroon. The case study chosen is the cocoa plantations of the Eton, an area close to Yaoundé.

370 **Subsistence activity in five villages on and around Mount Cameroon in Victoria Division, West Cameroon.**
Geoffrey M. D. Guillaume, Sanford H. Bederman. Atlanta,
Georgia: Georgia State College, 1967. 33p. 10 maps. bibliog.
(School of Arts and Sciences Research Papers, no. 14).
This is a detailed study of the physical environment and subsistence activity of five villages within the Mount Cameroon area: Masuma, Upper Buasa, Bona Ngombe, Kongwe, and Mobende. The physical, historical, and economic settings of the five villages are presented. A special section contributed by Nicholas Freville describes nutrition and health in subsistence communities in the forest areas of Mount Cameroon.

371 **Family and farm in Southern Cameroon.**
Jane I. Guyer. Boston, Massachusetts: African Studies Center,
Boston University, 1984. 154p. 2 maps. bibliog. (African Research
Studies, no. 15).
The author presents African family history and agricultural history as 'interactive processes.' More precisely, Beti women's farming of the *afub owondo* (groundnut fields) in Southern Cameroon is analysed. Salient issues presented are the centrality of gender in understanding the historical evolution of African production; the importance of the dynamics of domestic, state, and other levels of power; and the necessity of understanding the changing structure of individual

options and the social processes of adjustment, negotiation, and struggle. The study is based on intensive field research.

372 **Hodogway (Cameroun nord): un village de montagne en bordure de plaine.** (Hodogway (North Cameroon): a mountain village at the plain's edge.)
Antoinette Hallaire. Paris; the Hague: Mouton, 1971. 79p.
4 maps. bibliog. (Atlas des Structures Agraires au Sud du Sahara, no. 6).

This is an extremely detailed analysis of mountain agriculture as practiced in Hodogway, a village in Northern Cameroon. The volume examines pertinent questions such as: What are the salient aspects of mountain agriculture? How do these systems enter into contact with the national monetary economy? What are the effects and how does a people react to these contacts and subsequently the end of their relative economic isolation? Four desk size maps graphically display the types of crops grown, methods of cultivation, owners, and the different groups of individuals who work specific plots of land in Hodogway. Other volumes in this series include J. Tissandier, *Zengoaga: étude d'un village Camerounais et de son terroir au contact forêt-savane* (Paris: Mouton, 1969. 88p. maps. bibliog.) and J. Champaud, *Mom, terroir Bassa (Cameroun)* (Paris: Mouton, 1973. 60p. maps. bibliog.).

373 **ZOGID (Zone of Guided Integrated Development): a research contribution to rural development.**
Philip Langley. Douala, Cameroon: Panafrican Institute for Development, 1982. 167p. 13 maps. bibliog. (Pedagogy and Methodology of Development Series).

A laboratory Zone for Guided Integrated Development (ZOGID) was established in the South West Province of Cameroon to examine the dynamic processes involved in rural development. Two questions which formed the basis of the study were: 'How can the training of development staff be improved by a feedback from research activity?'; and 'Can the research process act as a catalyst for development activities in a small-sized rural area?' A basic description of ZOGID is followed by discussion of the problems and promises of the programme, feedback and local initiatives, improving the training programme, and a debate on regional development strategies.

374 **The design of rural development: lessons from Africa.**
Uma Lele, foreword by Robert S. McNamara. Baltimore, Maryland; London: Johns Hopkins University Press, 1975. 276p. 9 maps. bibliog.

Published for the World Bank, this volume examines rural development policies and programmes in sub-Saharan Africa with the aim of finding out how to raise the productivity of the rural poor. The author discusses the nature of production systems in Africa, agricultural extension and mass participation, agricultural credit, the marketing of agricultural output, basic social services, and training for rural development. Especially interesting is a section entitled 'Forms of rural

evelopment administration' which examines 'autonomous' development projects
and 'nationally' planned programmes. An appendix provides project reviews for
Cameroon, Ethiopia, Kenya, Malawi, Mali, Nigeria, and Tanzania.

375 **La place du coton dans la vie des paysans du Nord-Cameroun.** (The
place of cotton in the life of the peasants of Northern Cameroon.)
Régine Levrat. *Les Cahiers d'Outre-Mer*, no. 145 (Jan.-March
1984), p. 33-62.
A major development effort has been placed on small-holder cotton production in
the North in recent years.

376 **Foreign aid and its role in maintaining the exploitation of the
agricultural sector: evidence from a case study in Africa.**
Claudio Shuftan. *International Journal of Health Services* vol. 13,
no. 1 (1983), p. 33-49. bibliog.
The author argues that even though most foreign aid donors are committed to
rural development in Third World nations, local governments which distribute
foreign aid are not equally committed to the principle. Furthermore, most Third
World nations expropriate the surpluses produced by agriculture and invest them
in other sectors of the economy. It is hypothesized that because of these two
factors 'foreign aid directed toward rural development is actually filling the
investment gap left by an internal system of unequal returns to production in
agriculture . . . indirectly financing the development of the other sectors of the
economy, even if this result is unintended.' Shuftan worked for USAID in
Cameroon.

377 **Le bassin Camerounais de la Bénoué et sa pêche.** (The Cameroon
basin of the Benoue and its fishing.)
Alfred Stauch. Paris: ORSTOM, 1966. 152p. maps. bibliog.
This is a study of the fishing industry of the Benoue River area.

378 **Inventaire des ressources du Nord du Cameroun, Afrique.**
(Inventory of resources of the north of Cameroon, Africa.)
United States. Department of Agriculture. France. Fonds d'Aide
et de Coopération. Washington DC: US Government Printing
Office, 1978. 190p. 7 maps. bibliog.
This study was commissioned to provide the basis for development planning of
livestock in North Cameroon. Information on a wide variety of human, livestock,
and other natural resources is presented. A more recent study of agriculture in
the North is contained in A. Hallaire, H. Frechou and Y. Marguerat's 'Les
activitiés, in *Le nord du Cameroun: des hommes, une région*, (Paris: ORSTOM,
1984, p. 375-494).

Le Cameroun fédéral. (Federal Cameroon.)
See item no. 9.

Agriculture and Animal Husbandry

L'Economie de l'ouest-Africain: perspectives de développement. (The economy of West Africa: perspectives on development.)
See item no. 320.

Cameroon: an export market profile.
See item no. 321.

Complexes agro-industriels au Cameroun. (Agro-industrial complexes in Cameroon.)
See item no. 351.

The Cameroons Development Corporation: partner in national growth.
See item no. 352.

Cooperatives

379 Banana co-operatives in the Southern Cameroons.
Shirley Ardener. *Proceedings of the Nigerian Institute of Social and Economic Research, Conference, December 1958.* Ibadan, Nigeria: NISER, 1959, p. 10-25.

During the 1950s a phenomenal growth of cooperative organizations took place in anglophone Cameroon in conjunction with a rise in peasant production of bananas. In the 1960s the banana boom ended and the cooperatives based on it largely died out. See also *The demise of the commercial banana industry in West Cameroon*, (q.v.).

380 Credit for the common man in Cameroon.
Mark W. DeLancey. *Journal of Modern African Studies*, vol. 15, no. 2 (1977), p. 316-22.

The rapid growth of the credit union movement is related to the quality of leadership, external support, tactical decisions, and a 'positive' environment – a strong desire to save and a widespread familiarity with relevant traditional institutions.

381 Institutions for the accumulation and redistribution of savings among migrants.
Mark W. DeLancey. *Journal of Developing Areas*, vol. 12, no. 2 (Jan. 1978), p. 209-24.

Investigation of both modern and traditional savings institutions as well as study of attitudes about saving money indicate that Third World populations may be able to contribute more capital for development than is usually assumed. A variety of cooperative structures support this propensity to save in Cameroon.

Cooperatives

382 **Savings and credit institutions in rural West Africa.**
Edited by Mark W. DeLancey. *Rural Africana*, new series no. 2
(Fall 1978), 115p. bibliog.
Most of the essays in this issue are relevant to Cameroon. Articles include: Mark
W. DeLancey's 'Savings and credit institutions in rural West Africa: introduc-
tion;' Virginia DeLancey's 'Women at the Cameroon Development Corporation
how their money works'; Steven Haggblade's 'Africanization from below: the
evolution of Cameroonian savings societies into western-style banks'; Hans F
Illy's 'How to build in the germs of failure: credit cooperatives in French
Cameroon'; and S. J. Epale's 'The mobilization of capital in a rural milieu: the
example of the Bakweri of the South-West Province of Cameroon.' Virginia
DeLancey's essay has been reprinted in *Rural financial markets in developing
countries*, edited by J. D. Von Pischke, D. W. Adams and G. Donald (Baltimore,
Maryland: Johns Hopkins University Press, 1983, p. 138-47).

383 **The US Peace Corps program for credit union and cooperative
development in Cameroon, 1969-1976.**
Mark W. DeLancey. *Studies in Comparative International
Development*, vol. 17, nos. 3-4 (Fall-Winter 1982), p. 92-123.
bibliog.
Field research was conducted in 1976 to analyse the results, outline the problems
and provide recommendations for changes in the Peace Corps programme to
assist cooperatives and credit unions. The Peace Corps has been very active in the
Cameroon cooperatives and rural development programme. Other forms of
intervention in the cooperative movement are examined in E. Kamdem's essay in
People's participation in development in black Africa, edited by A. C.
Mondjanagni (Paris: Karthala, 1984, p. 324-36).

384 **Die Genossenschaften in Kamerun: ihre Entwicklung und ihre
Bedeutung für die wirtschaftliche und soziale Entwicklung des
Landes.** (Cooperatives in Cameroon: their development and
importance for economic and social development of the country.)
Ekkehart Gabelmann. Marburg an der Lahn, GFR:
Eukerdruck, 1971. 270p. maps. bibliog. (Marburger Schriften zum
Genossenschaftswesen, vol. B, no. 7).
This is the most significant study of cooperatives in Cameroon. Though it is now
dated, it remains an important work on the history and development of the
cooperative movement.

385 **The provident societies in the rural economy of Yaoundé, 1945-
1960.**
Jane I. Guyer. Brookline, Massachusetts: Boston University,
African Studies Center, 1980. 18p. (Working Paper, no. 37).
The 'Société Indigène de Prévoyance' (Native Provident Society) from 1937 to the
early 1960s was the main instrument of rural development policy of French
colonial administration. The purpose of this article is to outline the economic

policies of the Provident Society in the Circumscription of Nyong-et-Sanaga
around the capital city of Yaoundé) in an effort to elucidate the Provident
Society's long-term impact on local economic structures and compare its
experience with other areas of Cameroon. The author asserts that both issues deal
with the interaction of peasant economies and state policies in African history.

386 **Brauchen Genossenschaften in Entwicklungsländern ein
Vermarktungsmonopol?** (Do cooperatives in developing countries
need a marketing monopoly?)
Hans F. Illy. *Zeitschrift für das Gesamte Genossenschaftswesen*,
vol. 21, no. 4 (1971), p. 361-74.

This analysis of UCCAO, the Union of Cameroon Arabica Coffee Cooperatives,
is based on extensive field research. UCCAO is the most successful cooperative
enterprise in Cameroon. A brief analysis in French is provided by Jacques
Champaud, in 'Coopératives et développement: l'UCCAO,' *Cahiers d'Outre-Mer*,
no. 85 (1969), p. 95-100. maps.

387 **Saving and credit system of the Bamileke in Cameroun – a study on
the internal financing of development.**
Hans F. Illy. In: *Development policy in Africa*. Edited by J. Voss.
Bonn; Bad Godesberg, GFR: Verlag Neue Gesellschaft: 1973, p.
293-314; 339-49.

Illy analyses traditional concepts of and institutions for saving money in Bamileke
society. He then considers the implications of this for Cameroon development
policy, especially the role of cooperative savings institutions. The 'tontine' or
'njangi,' a traditional institution, is compared to the Coopératives de Crédit
Mutuel established by French colonialists. The failure of the latter is examined.

388 **Savings associations among the Bamileke: traditional and modern
cooperation in South West Cameroon.**
Dan Soen, Patrice de Comarmond. *Zeitschrift für Ethnologie*,
vol. 96, no. 2 (1971), p. 145-54.

This comparison of traditional and modern cooperative savings societies is one of
several essays on this topic published by Soen and de Comarmond. Bamileke
savings societies have provided capital for much of the commerce for which the
Bamileke are so famous.

Education

389 Conseil de l'Enseignement Supérieur et de la Recherche Scientifique et Technique. (Council of Higher Education and Scientific and Technical Research.)
Cameroon, Conseil de l'Enseignement Supérieur et de la Recherche Scientifique et Technique. Yaoundé: Centre d'Edition et de Production de Manuels et d'Auxiliaires de l'Enseignement, 1974. 115p.

A collection of decrees, reports, and speeches concerning the creation and functions of the Conseil de l'Enseignement Supérieur et de la Recherche Scientifique et Technique in Cameroon. The volume outlines the needs that the Conseil is to serve as well as the guidance that it must give to the fostering of higher education in Cameroon.

390 The Africanization of the labor market: educational and occupational segmentations in the Camerouns.
Remi Clignet. Los Angeles; London: University of California Press, 1976. 230p. map.

The author examines education as a determinant of occupational placement and achievement within the process of Africanization of the labour market in Cameroon. Because of significant differences in the organizational characteristics of enterprises existing in Cameroon as well as the difference in worker profiles (manual versus nonmanual workers), the influence of the educational variable as determining entry into the labour force, access to higher skill levels, and level of income is seen as being culturally related.

391   **Educational and occupational differentiation in a new country: the case of the Cameroun.**
Remi Clignet. *Economic Development and Cultural Change*, vol. 25, no. 4 (July 1977), p. 731-46.
Sharp differences exist in the profile and determinants of occupational achievement among manual and nonmanual labourer populations in Cameroon. The author claims that this disproves the initial assumptions made by social scientists and planners that minimized the existence and implications of cleavages in social structures and processes.

392   **Teachers and national values in Cameroon: an inferential analysis from census data.**
Remi Clignet. In: *Values, identities and national integration*. Edited by J. N. Paden.   Evanston, Illinois: Northwestern University Press, 1980, p. 321-36.
This chapter examines various demographic attributes of teachers in Cameroon which may aid in predicting their potential contribution to the modernization and integration of the nation. The first section describes the degree to which the social and ethnic background of teachers differs from that of the urban population at large, and varies across sectors. The second section examines the specific life-styles of the numerous subpopulations involved in the comparison.

393   **Education and sexual inequality in Cameroon.**
Brian Cooksey. *Journal of Modern African Studies*, vol. 20, no. 1 (March 1982), p. 167-77.
The article is concerned 'with education as a specific locus of sexual inequality' in Cameroon. Brief sections discuss sex, school enrollment, and performance in Cameroon, school performance in Yaoundé and the Centre-South province, examination performance, and patterns of secondary school entry.

394   **Education in anglophone Cameroon, 1915-1975.**
Christiane Courade, Georges Courade, translated by Ch. Chouvet, G. Ndeby, Taku J. Enow.   Yaoundé: ONAREST, 1977. 78p. 13 maps. (Travaux et Documents de l'Institut des Sciences Humaines, no. 3).
The first half of the book describes the development of educational policy in West Cameroon from 1915 to 1975. Inclusive in the analysis is a description of the precolonial, immediate postcolonial, and present day educational systems. The second half of the book outlines the impact that schools and education in general have had on West Cameroon. An index provides a chronology of education and a statistical analysis of the scholarized population (1917-1947) within the territory.

Education

395 **A case for early bilingualism.**
Bernard Fonlon. *Abbia* (Yaoundé), no. 4 (Dec. 1963), p. 56-94.
This is an important essay in the on-going disputes over the choice of a national
language and the choice of a language (or languages) for educational purposes.

396 **The genuine intellectual.**
Bernard Fonlon. Yaoundé: Buma Kor, 1978. 152p.
Dr. Fonlon is one of Cameroon's leading scholars, but he has also been deeply
engaged in politics. Although long a member of the CNU he has also been known
as an independent thinker and one willing to argue against establishment policies.
In this brief essay, Fonlon discusses the roles he sees as proper for universities
and students in developing countries. It poses such questions as What is an
intellectual? What is his role in society? Why does there seem to be a shortage of
such individuals in Africa? The essay is directed to Cameroon and other African
students and it has been widely read in Cameroon.

397 **Community education and community development in Cameroon:
the British colonial experience, 1922-1961.**
Emil Molindo Kwo. *Community Development Journal: An
International Forum*, vol. 19, no. 4 (Oct. 1984), p. 204-13.

398 **Federal Republic of Cameroon.**
Victor T. LeVine, Henri M'ballah. In: *The educated African: a
country by country survey of educational development in Africa.*
Edited by Helen Kitchen. New York: Praeger, 1962, p. 519-32.
map. bibliog.
Educational development and the system of education are the major topics.
Separate sections are presented for the anglophone and francophone sectors.

399 **Social differentiation and regional disparities: educational
development in Cameroon.**
Jean-Yves Martin. In: *Regional disparities in educational
development: diagnosis and policies for reduction.* Edited by G.
Carron, Ta Ngoc Châu. Paris: UNESCO, International Institute
for Educational Planning, 1980, p. 23-113. 8 maps. bibliog.
The study attempts to clarify the processes and causes which foster social
differentiation and regional disparities of educational development in Cameroon.
References are also made to the educational development experiences of Chad
and Nigeria. The first section presents the historical dimension and regional
context of disparities in Cameroon. The second section analyses the regional
disparities in education. Finally, an examination is made of regional disparities
and social inequalities.

400 **Education and manpower. The economic potential of West Cameroon, priorities for development, vol. 7.**
Edward A. Podesta. Menlo Park, California: Stanford Research Institute, 1965. 195p. map.
Primary and secondary education, teacher training, vocational and commercial education, and the Cameroon College of Arts, Science and Technology (CCAST) are discussed. A brief history of education and an attempt at manpower forecasting are included.

401 **St. Joseph's College Sasse-Buea: a brief history (1939-1981).**
Sasse Old Boys Association. Victoria, Cameroon: Sasse Old Boys Association, 1981. 99p.
This concise history of St. Joseph's College, the first secondary school established in anglophone Cameroon, presents in chronological order the establishment and expansion of the school, highlighting important historical events connected with its growth. It is this school which for ten years was the sole supplier of typists, clerks, and fieldworkers for the colonial government, the Native Administration, and the Cameroon Development Corporation (CDC). Since independence, the school has produced graduates which are found in almost every occupational field. Included is a list of all individuals who were admitted into the programme from 1939 to 1981.

402 **Conflict and culture in African education: authority patterns in a Cameroonian lycée.**
Michael G. Schatzberg. *Comparative Education Review*, vol. 23 (Feb. 1979), p. 52-65.
The thesis of the article is that the daily life and administration of the lycée was hindered by faculty members' differing perceptions of authority relationships, largely due to the fact that they were socialized by vastly different cultures, namely, French and British.

403 **Education in Cameroon.**
Soloman Shu. In: *Education in Africa: a comparative survey*. Edited by A. Babs Fafunwa, J. U. Aisiku. Boston, Massachusetts: Allen & Unwin, 1982, p. 28-48.
The author provides a summary of education in Cameroon. Separate sections describe the historical development, organization, administration, control, curriculum, and financing of all levels of Cameroon education. A short appendix provides useful annual statistics of pupils and teachers in schools from 1969 to 1970, and from 1978 to 1979.

404 **Focus on official bilingualism in Cameroon: its relationship to education.**
Gisele Tchoungi. In: *A sociolinguistic profile of urban centers in Cameroon.* Edited by Edna L. Koenig, Emmanuel Chia, John Povey. Los Angeles: Crossroads Press, 1983, p. 93-115.
The author finds bilingualism to be a failure as a policy and a disaster for the education system. She argues that at least a part of the child's education should be done in a Cameroon language.

405 **Language, schools, and government in Cameroon.**
H. O. H. Vernon-Jackson. New York: Teachers College Press, Columbia University, 1967. 31p. bibliog.
The author presents the historical foundations of foreign language introduction into Cameroon and the subsequent effect this has had on school and national language policies. The assertion is made that 'the language problems of the government official and the educator meet in the school.' Furthermore, when differences arise in policy between the government official and the educator, the former is said to prevail. A general survey is first made of Cameroon's early languages before the establishment of formally organized schools. A description of the mission period (1844-1884) is followed by a brief explication of the language policies fostered by the German, French, and British colonial powers. In addition, the early language policies of the newly independent Cameroon Federal Republic are examined.

406 **Bilan de scolarisation dans les montagnes Mofu, Nord Cameroun.**
(Evaluation of education in the Mofu Mountains of North Cameroon.)
J. Vincent. *Cahiers ORSTOM, Série Sciences Humaines*, vol. 16, no. 4 (1979), p. 305-28.
Migration, occupational, and religious status are examined as variables among 1,400 primary school children. Qualifications, rather than mere attendance at school, influence migration.

ZOGID (Zone of Guided Integrated Development): a research contribution to rural development.
See item no. 373.

Cultural policy in the United Republic of Cameroon.
See item no. 407.

UNESCO Statistical Yearbook.
See item no. 462.

Africa prospect: progress in education.
See item no. 466.

Art and Music

407 **Cultural policy in the United Republic of Cameroon.**
J. C. Bahoken, Engelbert Atangana.   Paris: UNESCO Press,
1976. 91p.

The purpose of this general series is to show how UNESCO member states plan
and apply their cultural policy. The primary emphasis of the series is on exploring
the technical aspects of cultural policy. The present volume is divided into five
parts which include Cameroon's ethnocultural framework, the institutional
framework of its cultural development, the cultural policy of Cameroon today,
indigenous artists and writers, and public and private cultural activity.

408 **Handbook of West African art.**
William R. Bascom, Paul Gebauer, Robert F.
Ritzenthaler.   Milwaukee, Wisconsin: Public Museum, 1953. 83p.
2 maps. bibliog.

The first half of this volume discusses the arts of the coastal region of West Africa
from Sierra Leone to anglophone Cameroon. The second half, prepared by Paul
Gebauer, is on the art of British Cameroons, including all of that portion of the
Trust Territory that joined the Republic of Cameroon and a small part of the
portion that joined Nigeria. Gebauer was a Baptist missionary who spent many
years in anglophone Cameroon, but he was also a devoted and skilled
anthropologist whose various studies and publications are an important contribution to our knowledge of anglophone Cameroon. In this essay he distinguishes
four areas of art, namely, Forest, Cross River, Grasslands, and Northern. The
latter is now part of Nigeria. In spite of the title of the book, most of the
discussion is of wood carving, with brief mention of ivory and brass. Other art
forms are not discussed. Black and white photographs are included.

Art and Music

409 **African music: a people's art.**
Francis Bebey, translated by Josephine Bennett. Westport,
Connecticut: Lawrence Hill, 1975. 145p. bibliog. Paris: Horizons
de France, 1969.

Francis Bebey was born in Douala in 1929. He is famous as a musician, as a
novelist, and as a student of music. In this introduction to African music he
examines forms, musicians, and instruments, as well as commenting on the role
and influence of music in African life. The emphasis is on traditional rather than
modern music. In addition to numerous photographs, there is an extensive
discography of African music organized by country of origin and type of music.

410 **Art and society in Africa.**
Richard Brain. London, New York: Longman, 1980. 304p.
bibliog.

The author attempts to discuss African art in its social context as well as presenting
a description of the art. He examines the religious symbolism of art, discusses art as
entertainment, and provides information on the artists and their materials. Much
ethnographic material is included. Although the volume discusses all of Africa
there are several large sections on Cameroon art. There are numerous black and
white photoraphs, but unfortunately, none in colour. The author has conducted
field work in Cameroon.

411 **L'Art traditionnel au Cameroun: statues et masques.** (Traditional
art in Cameroon: statues and masks.)
Joseph-Marie Essomba. Suresnes, France: Jean Dupuch, 1982.
93p.

The primary purpose of this study 'is to enable a large portion of the public to
discover the artistic patrimony kept in our museums in Cameroon.' Two short
sections examine the role and history of the National Museum of Yaoundé and
the Benedictine Museum of Mont-Febe. Exquisite colour photographs detail the
statuary and mask collections assembled within Cameroon. While the photo-
graphed statues are made of either bronze or wood, the masks discussed in the
text are made of wood, fibre, ivory or bronze. The text is in both English and French.

412 **Crafts and the arts of living in Cameroon.**
Jocelyne Etienne-Nugue, Harri Peccinotti. Baton Rouge,
Louisiana: Louisiana State University Press, 1982. 156p. map.

The volume 'reveals a remarkable artistry and ingenuity applied to tasks as
routine as the making of a roof or a chimney hood for a house, the carving and
shaping of a toy, the weaving of a basket, and the forming of a drum.' The first
section, entitled 'Nature and the hand of man' shows the unique craftwork
embodied in the construction of straw, earth, and stone dwellings. The second
section, 'Forms of everyday art' portrays the craft tradition in Foumban, the
artistry inherent in the making of basketry, calabash, and pottery, and the objects
that children make. The final section, 'Ornaments and festivals' presents the craft
of weavers and embroiderers, as well as that required for the *manifestation* of
Bamileke ceremonies. The text is accompanied by eighty exquisite (many full
page) colour photographs.

130

413 **Au Cameroun: weaving – tissage.** (In Cameroon: weaving-tissage.)
Venice Lamb, Alastain Lamb. Douala, Cameroon: Elf Serepca
Cameroun, 1981. 192p. 2 maps. bibliog.
An analysis is provided of the numerous weaving traditions of Cameroon through
a combination of extensive field research and the perusal of museum collections
and photographic archives both within and outside of the nation. Major sections
include a discussion of 'Ndop' cloths, the narrow strip horizontal treadle loom,
ground looms and vertical looms, raphia weaving, and old styles and new textiles.
The highly descriptive text, which is written in both French and English, is
accompanied by 278 colour and black and white photographs.

414 **L'Art et l'artisanat Africains.** (African art and artisans.)
Engelbert Mveng. Yaoundé: Editions CLE, 1980. 163p. bibliog.
Reverend Father Mveng, a professor in the Department of History at the
University of Yaoundé, is one of the foremost students of Cameroon art. He has
also undertaken considerable activities to foster the arts in Cameroon. While this
volume discusses African art in general, most of the examples and illustrations are
Cameroonian. There are numerous sketches and black and white photographs.
Ceramics; metallurgy; stonework and precious gems; wood, bark and other plant
materials; and animal products are discussed. The artist and his role in society is
considered.

415 **The art of Cameroon.**
Tamara Northern. Washington DC: Smithsonian Institute, 1984.
207p.
This museum catalogue is perhaps the most comprehensive work of its kind
concerning the artwork of Cameroon. Organized by the Smithsonian Institution
Traveling Exhibition Service (SITES), the exhibition which produced this volume
represented the first comprehensive showing of Cameroonian artwork in the
United States. The pieces were gathered from over twenty-three sources, foreign
and domestic, private and public, and were put on display at various locations
throughout the United States. The catalogue is divided between artwork of the
Grassfields and that of the forest areas. Over 250 black and white and colour
photographs portray aspects of Cameroonian artwork. Each photograph is
accompanied by a discussion of the object's origin, donator, and measurements as
well as by an extensive narrative.

416 **A guide to Cameroon art from the collection of Paul and Clara
Gebauer.**
Portland Art Museum, foreword by Francis J. Newton. Portland,
Oregon: Portland Art Museum, 1968. [not paginated]. map.
This is a unique museum guide of the private Cameroon art collection of Paul and
Clara Gebauer held at the Portland Art Museum from October 30 to December
1, 1968. Paul (a missionary of the American Baptist Missionary Society) and
Clara (artist and teacher) Gebauer lived and collected artwork in Cameroon
between 1931 and 1961. Various masks, stools, pipes, figures, baskets, and other
pieces of artwork are presented in black and white photographs accompanied by
explanatory texts. An index separates the pieces of artwork according to type and

region of origin (Bamum, Mambila, Northern Area, transitional Bamum Area, and Widekum).

417 **Nord Cameroun: montagnes et hautes terres.** (North Cameroon: mountains and highlands.)
Christian Seignobos. Roquevaire, France: Editions Parenthèses, 1982. 188p. maps. bibliog. (Collection Architectures Traditionelles).

This volume is a landmark in the study of traditional architecture in Northern Cameroon. The first half of the book discusses the specific types of architecture utilized in the mountainous Northern regions. Specific descriptions are made of varied topics such as the functioning of a mountaineer's farm and the effect that migration has had on architectural techniques. The second half describes the salient aspects of the various types of architecture found in the Northern highlands of Cameroon. Specific analyses are made of the architecture of the Southern Mandara hills and the habitats of the highlands south of the Benoue region. Detailed artistic renditions as well as black and white photographs graphically portray traditional Cameroonian architecture. Also see by the same author, 'L'Habitation' in *Le nord du Cameroun: des hommes, une région*, (Paris: ORSTOM, 1984, p. 181-202).

418 **Cameroon.**
Marcilene K. Wittmer. Charlotte, North Carolina: Mint Museum, 1977. 73p. map. bibliog.

This museum catalogue commemorates the second in a series of eight exhibitions of work from the William and Robert Arnett collection of African art. While the majority of the collection is from the Grasslands, also included are art pieces from the southern forests, northern perimeter, and Cross River region. One hundred and fifteen black and white stills present Cameroonian figures, masks, statues, pipes, drums, bowls, and stools.

A select bibliography of music in Africa.
See item no. 489.

A bibliography of African art.
See item no. 490.

Literature and Folklore

19 **The new Mongo Beti.**
Stephen H. Arnold. *Africana Journal*, vol. 13, no. 1-4 (1982), p. 111-23.

The article comments on Beti's 'suicide artistique' or lack of writing new novels in h 1960s until the appearance of *Remember Ruben* and *Perpétue ou l'habitude du malheur* in 1974. The author focuses on the new themes and subjects that Beti has emphasized since 1974. Short sections are entitled 'Documentary-historical fiction,' 'Influences of oral literature,' 'Leadership,' and 'The anti-neocolonial novel as revolutionary handbook.'

20 **Agatha Moudio's son.**
Francis Bebey, translated by Joyce A. Hutchinson. Nairobi, London, Ibadan: Heinemann Educational Books, 1971; Yaoundé: CLE, 1967. 154p.

The author is well-known in Cameroon not only as a writer, but also as a musician. In this novel we learn the story of Mbenda, a Douala youth who marries the woman his father has selected for him, but he continues to love his own choice, Agatha Moudio. This prize-winning novel shows, in a humorous fashion, some of the problems as African and European customs mix and conflict in Cameroon rural society.

21 **King Albert.**
Francis Bebey, translated by Joyce A. Hutchinson. Westport, Connecticut: Lawrence Hill, 1981; Yaoundé: CLE, 1976. 167p.

Political rivalry, the clash between the generations, and love are major factors in his argument for a blending of modernity and tradition in Cameroon society.

133

Literature and Folklore

422 **Die Volksdichtung der Wakweli: Sprichwörter, Fabeln, Märchen, Parabeln, Rätsel, und Lieder.** (The folklore of the Wakweli: proverbs, fables, tales, parables, riddles and songs.)
C. Bender. *Zeitschrift für Eingeborenen-Sprachen* 4 (1922), 122p.
This is a collection of Bakweri tales, proverbs, aphorisms, riddles and songs in the Kpe language and in German translation.

423 **King Lazarus.**
Mongo Beti. New York: Collier, 1971. 190p.
The story revolves around Essomba Mednouga, a healthy polygamous Bantu chief, who, in 1948 is stricken with 'satyriasis.' Essomba becomes temporarily insane and converts to Christianity, takes the name Lazurus, and discards his numerous wives save one. Beti wittily satirizes the Catholic Church, tribal customs, and French colonialism. The novel was first published under the title *Le roi miracule* (Paris: Editions Buchet-Chastel-Corréa, 1958.)

424 **Mission to Kala.**
Mongo Beti, translated by Peter Green, introduction by Bernth Lindfors. New York: Collier, 1971. 215p.; Paris: Editions Correa Buchet/Chastel, 1957; London: Frederick Muller, 1958.
The French edition of this book is titled *Mission terminée*. Beti, one of Cameroon's most famous writers, was born in 1932 in the Yaoundé region. He studied in Cameroon and France. In this novel he relates the story of a young man, educated in the urban setting of the university, who travels up-country in Cameroon. His trip is an education, both for him and for the rural villagers he meets.

425 **The poor Christ of Bomba.**
Mongo Beti, translated by Gerald Moore. London, Ibadan, Nairobi: Heinemann Educational Books, 1971. 219p.; Paris: Editions Robert Laffont, 1956.
Beti attacks the Christian missionary movement in Cameroon rather strongly in this volume. In so doing he points at both the frequent hypocrisy of the white missionary and the perverted purposes of the black convert. The story is based on the experiences of young Cameroon women who were put in special schools at Roman Catholic Missions to be trained for marriage and Christian life.

426 **Perpetua and the habit of unhappiness.**
Mongo Beti, translated by John Reed, Clive Wake. London: Heinemann, 1978. 219p.
This novel, first published as *Perpétue et l'habitude du malheur* (Paris: Buchet e Chastel, 1974), tells the story of a woman, Perpetua, who dies during childbirth Her brother, Essola, just out of prison, seeks the causes of her death. He uncovers the story, and concludes that unhappiness is the key factor.

27 Remember Ruben.
Mongo Beti, translated by Gerald Moore.   London, Nairobi:
Heinemann, 1980. 252p; Paris: Editions 10/18, 1974.

This is a novel of forced labour in a French African colony and of nationalist political activity after the Second World War. A trade union leader, Ruben, plays a role in the story though he is in the background. The main character, Mor Zamba, is arrested and tortured and eventually he goes into hiding. His party is banned by the colonial administration and guerilla war begins. Mor Zamba's story is presented against a background of the political history of the colony – a background strikingly similar to Cameroon's political evolution.

28 Les contes du Cameroun. (Tales of Cameroon.)
Charles Binam Bikoi, Emmanuel Soundjock.   Yaoundé: Centre
d'Edition et de Production de Manuels et d'Auxiliaires
d'Enseignement, 1977. 264p.

The purpose of this textbook is to introduce for the first time on a national scale Cameroon's previously unused rich oral literature into scholastic programmes. A total of twenty-four classic oral tales, such as 'The lion and the tortoise' and 'The leopard and the monkey' are reproduced in their entirety. Each text is followed by an explanation of the vocabulary employed, structure and general analysis of the tale, and its cultural significance for Cameroon.

29 Writing in French from Senegal to Cameroon.
A. C. Brench.   London: Oxford University Press, 1967. 153p.
bibliog.

The author presents a short and concise, yet comprehensive, overview of the French literary tradition evident in West Africa. Cameroon novels discussed include Ferdinand Oyono's works *Une vie de boy* and *Le vieux nègre et la médaille* and Mongo Beti's *Le roi miraculé*. A brief analysis of the literary significance of each author is followed by a four-to-six page extract from one of their acclaimed works. An appendix provides a brief historical sketch and bibliography of all items published for each author.

30 Because of women.
Mbella Sonne Dipoko.   London: Heinemann, 1970. 178p.
(African Writers Series, no. 57).

This novel centres around Ngoso, a womanizer who desires to have a large family. He faces a dilemma in choosing a wife in that he must pick between Ewudu, who is potentially barren, and Njale, who is pregnant with his child. Conflict arises when Njale is beaten and sent off by Ngoso because she accuses him of sleeping with his friend's wife. Upon hearing of Njale's death, Ngoso concentrates on securing the love of Ewudu – who also eventually leaves him.

31 A few days and nights.
Mbella Sonne Dipoko.   London: Heinemann, 1970. 184p.
(African Writers Series, no. 82).

Dipoko, although born in Douala, grew up in West Cameroon and Nigeria. He has studied in France, worked for the Nigerian Broadcasting Corporation, and was on the editorial staff of *Présence Africain*. The novel's description of a few days and nights details a crisis among four student friends living and working in Paris. One of the four, Thérèse, a young French girl of the bourgeois, wishes to marry Doumbe, a Cameroon student also of the group. Troubles begin when Thérèse's father attempts to prevent the relationship from continuing.

432 **L'Image du Cameroun dans la littérature coloniale Allemande.**
(The image of Cameroon in German colonial literature.)
Max F. Dippold. *Cahiers d'Etudes Africaines*, no. 49 (1973), p. 37-59.

German writers, administrators, and others involved with the colonies held variety of views and stereotypes about Cameroonians in general and selected ethnic groups in particular. Dippold draws these out of various publications.

433 **The orphan in Cameroon folklore and fiction.**
S. Domowitz. *Research in African Literatures*, vol. 12, no. 3 (1981), p. 350-58.

The orphan is an important character and the hero of many tales in the oral traditions of the Beti, Bassa and Bulu peoples of Cameroon. Furthermore, the orphan as a protagonist is found in numerous Cameroon novels by authors such as Ferdinand Oyono and Mongo Beti. The author therefore compares the modern classics of Oyono (*Un vie de boy*) and Beti (*Le pauvre Christ de Bomba*) to twenty-four Beti, Bassa and Bulu orphan tales to show how 'an understanding of the orphan's traditional role in the tales is essential to a more complete understanding of modern Cameroon writing.'

434 **The overloaded ark.**
Gerald M. Durrell. New York: Tower Publications, 1953. 251p.
London: Faber & Faber, 1963. 238p.

Durrell's books on his animal-gathering trips to Cameroon provide valuable insights on animal and human life as well as descriptive material on the geography of the country. Although some of his writings are on the required list for anglophone Cameroon secondary school students, many Cameroonians argue that Durrell presents a derogatory and embarrassing view of their country. This story chronicles a six month 'collecting trip' in Cameroon that the author made with John Yealland, a bird collector.

435 **The Bafut beagles.**
Gerald M. Durrell. New York: Tower Publications, 1954. 267p.

This fictional account of the author's travels in Cameroon relies on the local form of English (Pidgin) for much of its narration. Durrell has made several trips to Cameroon to gather animals for zoos in Europe. His books are widely read in Europe and America as well as in Cameroon, both for their discussion of wildlife and their portrayal of human life. In this volume he relates his experiences with the Fon (King) of Bafut and with his trackers. Excerpts from this book appear in *Harper's Magazine*.

436 **A zoo in my luggage.**
Gerald Durrell.   Harmondsworth, England: Penguin, 1964. 191p.
The author, a noted zoologist, chronicles a six-month trip made with his wife to
the Kingdom of Bafut, Cameroon. The purpose of the trip and the subject of the
book is the creation of the author's private zoo. Many Cameroon species are
discussed and there are numerous illustrations.

437 **The new Noah.**
Gerald Durrell.   Harmondsworth, England: Penguin, 1966. 204p.
The author describes the trials and tribulations as well as the excitement and
pleasure of observing and capturing animals in their native habitats. The book is
divided into three major sections entitled: 'Collecting in the Cameroons,' 'Hunts
and captures in Guiana,' and 'Perambulations in Paraguay.'

438 **The good foot.**
Nsanda Eba.   Ibadan: Oxford University Press, 1977. 149p.
The story revolves around the Elates and their son Mbamu who move from their
village of Ntem to the colonial-owned plantations in the southern portion of West
Cameroon. The description of 'Mbamu's life in the various social strata at the
village level, plantation level, primary school level and finally college level, gives
one an insight in the mode of living in West Cameroon then.'

439 **Miscellany of Maroua Fulfulde (Northern Cameroun).**
Paul Kazuhisa Eguchi.   Tokyo: Institute for the Study of
Languages and Cultures of Asia and Africa, Tokyo University of
Foreign Studies, 1974. vol. 1. 211p. map. bibliog. (African
Languages and Ethnography, I).
This important linguistic and anthropological study of the 'Humour et Sagesse
Peuls' is based on the oral traditions of the Fulbe people of Maroua, a group
located on the Diamare plain of Northern Cameroon. Specialized chapters
present Fulbe riddles, word category games, tongue-twisters, children's prose and
rhymes, and proverbs. Also included are chapters explicating Fulbe abusive and
embarrassing expressions, salutations, spells, and expressions of praise. All
examples are presented in the original Fulbe language with translations. Some
expressions, the meanings of which the author has not yet discovered, 'are
included as linguistic examples, in case they may be of use to other researchers.'

440 **Fulfulde tales of North Cameroon II.**
Paul Kazuhisa Eguchi.   Tokyo: Institute for the Study of
Languages and Cultures of Asia and Africa, 1980. 605p. bibliog.
(African Languages and Ethnography, XIII).
The compiler and translator of this volume collected the stories in Cameroon in
1960-70. Some fifty-six stories are presented in the Fulani language, (which is also
known as Fulfulde) and in English translation. Although these stories represent
an important contribution to the study of African oral literature, they also are
valuable as ethnography and history. The bibliography is an important source of
references to Japanese publications on Cameroon subject matter, some of which
are in English and some in Japanese.

137

441   **Criquets et vautours – mythes de migration et d'installation des Gemjek et Zulgo du Nord-Cameroun.** (Locusts and vultures – migration and installation myths of the Gemjek and Zulgo of North Cameroon.)
Charlotte de Graffenried.   *Genève-Afrique*, vol. 22, no. 2 (1984), p. 103-18.

The article discusses the oral traditions relating to the migrations of the Gemjek and Zulgo, two groups of the North Eastern section of Northern Cameroon' Mandara mountains. Different reasons for migrating, according to myth include lack of water, destruction of crops by drought or locusts, family feuds, escape from being captured as slaves, and fear of the actions of angry ancestors.

442   **The white man of god.**
Kenjo Jumban.   London: Heinemann, 1980. 151p. (African Writers Series, no. 231).

This is the story of Tansa, a child growing up in colonial Cameroon. The usual crises of growing up are made especially complex by the conflict between the African and European cultures and the demands of the Christian world, which are conveyed through a mission priest.

443   **Literary creativity in anglophone Cameroon.**
Curtis A. Keim, Karen R. Keim.   *Research in African Literatures*, vol. 13, no. 2 (May 1982), p. 216-22.

Cameroon is internationally known for its French-speaking writers, such as Mongo Beti and Ferdinand Oyono, but the nation's anglophone writers have not yet received the same international prestige. The article summarizes recent articles and the debate in Cameroon as to the reasons underpinning 'the paucity of literary creativity in anglophone Cameroon.'

444   **Popular fiction publishing in Cameroon.**
Karen R. Keim.   *African Book Publishing Record*, vol. 9, no. 1 (1983), p. 7-11.

After brief discussions of anglophone and francophone writers, Keim discusses in some detail the work of Naha Désiré.

445   **Adventuring with Jaja.**
Sankie Maimo.   Yaoundé: the author, 1976. 96p.

This reader was designed for instructional purposes and represents 'an attempt to provide the young at heart with a work of adventure with a strictly local background.' Real life problems, such as rising unemployment and corruption in high places, encourage Jaja to day-dream. A glossary at the end provides the reader with definitions of difficult English words and idioms, as well as English translations.

446 **Les chauves-souris.** (The bats.)
Bernard Nanga. Paris: Présence Africaine, 1980. 203p.

This is a story of post-independence politics in an unnamed African country, one which resembles Cameroon in many features. However, the novel is also a study of male and female roles in contemporary African society. It is an interesting novel, and it frequently hints – tantalizingly – at the Machiavellian aspects of Cameroon politics and economics. At times this book has been banned in Cameroon. The author is Cameroonian, born in 1934 near Yaoundé. He is presently teaching at the University of Yaoundé.

447 **Blasons Peuls: éloges et satires du Nord-Cameroun.** (Peul blasons: praises and satires of North Cameroon.)
Dominique Noye. Paris: Librairie Orientaliste Paul Geuthner, 1976. 192p.

This is a collection of fifty-nine poems collected orally from the Peul people, a group located in the Diamare district of Northern Cameroon. The author compares Peul oral poetry to a genre of sixteenth century French poetry entitled *blason*. *Blason* poetry is a highly descriptive form of art which entails either high, noteworthy praise or satire of a person or a subject. The poems, which are written in both French and Peul, are divided into three major groups: the 'animated,' 'animal,' and 'human' worlds.

448 **Houseboy.**
Ferdinand Oyono, translated by John Reed. London, Ibadan, Nairobi: Heinemann Educational Books, 1966. 140p. Also published as *Boy!* New York: Collier, 1970. 144p. with an introduction by Edris Makward.

This novel depicts basic elements of race relations in French Cameroon through the experiences of Toundi, a servant who works in the homes of various white colonial and mission personnel. Toundi passes from awe and admiration for the ways of the European to realization of the realities of European morality. His awakening leads to his death at the hands of the Europeans who feel he has come to know them too well. The author, a Cameroonian, was born in 1929, educated in France and Cameroon, and has worked in the Cameroon diplomatic service.

449 **The old man and the medal.**
Ferdinand Oyono, translated by John Reed. London: Heinemann, 1969. 167p. (African Writers Series, no. 39). First published as *Le vieux nègre et la médaille*. Paris: Editions Julliard, 1956.

Oyono satirizes French colonial rule in Cameroon and in general through the eyes of Meka, an old villager who unequivocally has supported the French presence. Because of Meka's model role under French rule – he donated all his land to the church, fought in the 'Great War,' and lost two sons in French wars – he is to receive a medal from France. Meka becomes disillusioned, however, when, despite his receipt of the medal, he is snubbed by the whites at the awards ceremony and is arrested and beaten for drunkenness and vagrancy.

450 **Three suitors: one husband and until further notice.**
Guillaume Oyono-Mbia. London: Methuen, 1968. 113p. First
published as *Trois prétendants: un Mari*. Yaoundé: Editions CLE,
1964.

These two plays are set in the Bulu village of Mvoutessi, Cameroon, *Three
suitors: one husband* was the first modern Cameroon play staged (in French) in
Yaoundé (1961). It is the story of a father who is attempting to get the best
possible bride price for his Western-educated daughter. His daughter, however,
schemes in order to marry the man she loves. *Until further notice* is about a family
waiting for the return of a daughter who has married a prestigious and powerful
government official. The primary theme of both plays is the inherent tension
between the traditional rural extended family and the individualism of the modern
urban dweller.

451 **Jusqu'à nouvel avis.** (Until further notice.)
Guillaume Oyono-Mbia. Yaoundé: Editions CLE, 1978. 48p.

This one act comedy is the story of a Europeanized African couple who return to
their native Cameroon. Their family and friends, expecting to reap the fruits of
the couples' prestigious position, are chagrined when the couple refuses to even
visit them. Two opposing conceptions of life create an abyss which separates the
couple from their friends and relatives.

452 **Le caméléon suivi de les épouses stériles.** (The chameleon followed
by the sterile wives.)
Patrice Ndedi Penda. Yaoundé: CLE, 1981. 116p.

This volume contains two plays in which the author attacks social problems he
observes in Cameroon society.

453 **Le livre Camerounais et ses auteurs.** (The Cameroon book and its
authors.)
Rene Philombe. Yaoundé: Les Editions Semences Africaines,
1983. 340p.

An excellent overview of Cameroon literature. The first section describes the
salient aspects of Cameroon literature, with the second section analysing crucial
problems and theories. The final section contains a comprehensive sixty-nine page
bibliographical summary of Cameroon authors.

454 **Kaningou ou les affres de l'alliance inversée.** (Kaningou or the
misfortunes of inverted alliance.)
Charles-Henry Pradelles de Latour Dejean. *L'Homme*, vol. 21,
no. 2 (April-June 1981), p. 103-13.

The author provides a unique interpretation of Kaningou, a well-known Bamileke
myth. Employing kinship data, the trials and tribulations of Kaningou are
discussed in terms of marriage alliance and birth rite symbolism.

A bibliography of Cameroun folklore.
See item no. 487.

Cuisine

455　**Le grand livre de la cuisine Camerounaise.** (The complete book of
Cameroon cuisine.)
Jean Grimaldi, Alexandrine Bikia.　Yaoundé: Edicam, [1981?].
259p. 5 maps.
This recipe book provides an extensive coverage of Cameroon cooking. Firstly,
400 recipes are provided for preparing primary ingredients such as bananas, rice,
fish and meat. This is followed by a presentation of the customs and manners
which preside at the preparation of food in the various provinces. Included are a
list of recipes and the specific ingredients utilized in each province. The principal
ingredients of Cameroon cooking (divided by scientific and generic labels) are
denoted by photographs, drawings, and short descriptive texts. The work also
contains a lexicon of various ingredients outlined according to French, scientific,
and indigenous vernacular terms. A glossary provides an alphabetized list of all
the recipes described within the cookbook for easy and quick reference.

456　**Auntie Kate's cookery book.**
K. E. Idowu.　London: Macmillan Education, 1982. 188p.
This collection of recipes and standard dishes from all corners of Cameroon, is a
must for all those interested in African cooking in general and that of Cameroon
in particular. 'Auntie Kate' introduces the recipes with a section on nutrition,
covering nutritional food groups, planning meals, and suggested menus, and a
chapter entitled 'To help you cook.' In this section, there is a general description
of weights and measures, culinary terms, kitchen equipment, and methods of
cooking in order to facilitate the preparation of the recipes provided. Recipes are
grouped under the following sub-headings: fish, stocks, soups, stews and sauces;
kokis and dibombas; foofoo; all-in-one-pot dishes (pottages); vegetable and
carbohydrate dishes) desserts and sweets; bread, cakes, pastries and biscuits;
preserves, fruit syrups, squashes and juices; beverages; and foods in season. An
earlier version of this book was published in Cameroon in 1976.

Statistics

457 Demographic Yearbook.
New York: United Nations, 1948- . annual.
Official statistics, though often of questionable validity, are presented on a variety
of demographic matters.

458 Tableaux économiques du Cameroun. (Cameroon economic
tables.)
Yves Morel. Douala, Cameroon: Collège Libermann, 1978.
232p.
One-hundred and forty-seven tables present data on human resources, communication, foreign commerce, prices, the budget, planning, and monetary matters. A
revised and updated version is expected.

**459 Geographical Distribution of Financial Flows to Developing
Countries.**
OECD. Paris: OECD-. annual.
This comprehensive statistical series elucidates the sources of external financial
resources for individual developing nations in terms of net and gross disburse-
ments, commitments, debt, debt service, and terms. The data provides the
researcher with financial resources allotted to a particular nation (in this case,
Cameroon) by Development Assistance Committee (DAC) member nations
(individually or by group), multilateral agencies, the Organization of Petroleum
Exporting Countries (OPEC), and the Council for Mutual Economic Assistance
(CMEA).

460   **The Statesman's Yearbook: Statistical and Historical Annual of the States of the World.**
    London: Macmillan, 1864- . annual.
Country-by-country statistics on an extensive range of subjects, including politics, economics, demography, education, health, defence, and other topics.

461   **Statistical Yearbook.**
    New York: United Nations, Statistical Office, 1948- . annual.
Provides a range of statistical data from all members of the UN.

462   **UNESCO Statistical Yearbook.**
    UNESCO.   Paris: UNESCO, 1963- . annual.
A wide range of data on education, publishing, and other modes of communication are presented.

Publishing, Broadcasting and the Press

463 The press of Africa: persecution and perseverance.
Frank Barton. London: Macmillan, 1979. 304p.
Press censorship is widespread in Africa and Cameroon is no exception. This study analyses censorship and intimidation of the press. The Cameroon Press Law of 1966 which was modified in June 1981 lays down the regulations under which newspapers, magazines and periodicals are either authorized or prohibited.

464 Presse écrite et développement politique au Cameroun. (Written press and political development in Cameroon.)
Jean-François Bayart. *Revue Française d'Etudes Politiques Africaines*, 88 (April 1973), p. 48-63.
Bayart examines the relationship between development of the press and political development in Cameroon.

465 Cameroon Tribune.
Yaoundé: 1974- . daily.
This is Cameroon's only major daily newspaper. It is government controlled, is published in French and has a circulation of about 20,000 copies. An English edition is published once a week. The press in Cameroon has had to endure a number of difficulties including high production costs and expensive paper, as well as both a dearth of revenue from advertising and low circulations. Non-government owned newspapers, such as the *Cameroon Times*, *Cameroon Outlook* and *La Gazette* suffer from censorship and other government imposed difficulties.

466 Africa prospect: progress in education.
Richard Greenough. Paris: UNESCO, 1966. 111p.
This volume includes a brief description (p. 89-95) of a textbook publishing company establshed by UNESCO in Yaoundé.

144

467 **The book in francophone Africa: a critical perspective.**
Gunter Simon. *African Book Publishing Record*, vol. 10, no. 4
(1984), p. 209-15.
Editions CLE, a religious publishing company in Yaoundé, is one of the examples
cited in this article.

468 **The book trade of the world. Vol. IV: Africa.**
Edited by Sigfred Tauber, Peter Weidhaas.   Munich: K. G. Saur,
1984. 391p.
Information on the publishing and bookselling industries is provided for each
country.

469 **World communications: a 200-country survey of press, radio,
television and film.**
Paris: UNESCO;   Epping, Essex, England: Gower; New York:
Unipub, 1975. 533p. bibliog.
This reference work includes a section on Cameroon which describes the key
aspects of the nation's press, news agencies, radio, film, space communications
and professional training and associations.

470 **The African book publishing record.**
Edited by Hans M. Zell.   Munich: Hans Zell and K. G. Saur,
1974- . quarterly.
It is the intent of the editor to provide bibliographic information and reviews of
all significant publishing from the African continent. Cameroon publications are
regularly covered. Author, title, and subject indexes are included.

471 **The African book world and press: a directory.**
Hans M. Zell, Carol Bundy.   Oxford, England: Hans Zell, 1983.
313p.
This third edition presents detailed information on the press and the publishing
industry.

472 **Publishing and book development in Africa: a bibliography.**
Hans M. Zell.   Paris: UNESCO, 1984. 143p. bibliog.
'The present bibliography is intended to focus attention on the growing African
book industry and to facilitate and encourage further research . . . .'

UNESCO Statistical Yearbook.
See item no. 462.

Museums, Archives and Libraries

473 The national archives of Cameroon.
Ralph A. Austen. *History in Africa*, vol. 1 (1974), p. 153-55.
This brief note, although now dated, describes the archival holdings (English, French and German) of Cameroon.

474 Libraries in West Africa: a bibliography.
Helen Davies.   Oxford, England: Hans Zell; Munich: K. G. Saur, 1982. 170p.
A variety of subjects are covered in this survey of libraries in sixteen countries.

475 Etudes Camerounaises, no. 52 (June 1956), 55p. bibliog.
This special issue on museums provides some material on a number of institutions, including the museums at Douala, Bamum, Diamaré and others.

476 National union list of African development plans, censuses and statistical abstracts.
Victoria K. Evalds.   Oxford, England: Hans Zell, 1985. 180p.
'This list brings together the combined holdings of the collections in twelve major US research libraries of government documents concerned with African development plans, censuses and statistical abstracts.'

477 African archives: Cameroon, Gambia, Sierra Leone.
David E. Gardinier, H. Gailey.   *Africana Newsletter*, vol. 1 (Summer 1963), p. 37-39.
The Yaoundé archives contain German and French colonial as well as Cameroon government materials. Some British colonial materials are kept there, but the best collection of these is in the Buea archives.

478 **Catalogue des archives coloniales Allemandes du Cameroun.**
(Catalogue of the German colonial archives of Cameroon.)
Eldridge Mohammadou. Yaoundé: Société Camerounaise
d'Histoire, 1972. 284p.

This is a catalogue of German colonial archives found and preserved by the
National Archives Service of Yaoundé. Documents with specific titles are
presented in German and followed by a French translation, with other
annotations being merely presented in French. The first half of the catalogue is a
general survey of German colonial documents arranged under subject headings.
The second half is an analytical survey of the archival documents with an
emphasis on those which pertain to Northern Cameroon. The four major
subheadings of this section are exploration and conquest, residences of
Adamawa, stations of Adamawa, and technical dossiers.

L'Art traditionel au Cameroun: statues et masques. (Traditional art in
Cameroon: statues and masks.)
See item no. 411.

The art of Cameroon.
See item no. 415.

A guide to Cameroon art from the collection of Paul and Clara Gebauer.
See item no. 416.

Cameroon.
See item no. 418.

147

Bibliographies

479 Bibliography of West Cameroon: economic development literature.
Menlo Park, California: Stanford Research Institute, 1965. 67p.
bibliog. (The Economic Potential of West Cameroon: Priorities for
Development, Supplement No. 2).

The bibliography is a supplement to the Stanford Research Institute's report *The
economic potential of West Cameroon – priorities for development*, (q.v.). The
primary objectives of the report are to denote relevant development planning
literature for West Cameroon and to aid the central government in the
development process. The bibliography includes 602 citations which are arranged
alphabetically under twenty-two separate sub-headings. Sources cited are from
the pre-1965 period in Cameroon development literature. A useful appendix cites
the significant events affecting the economic development of West Cameroon up
to 1965.

480 German Africa: a select annotated bibliography.
Jon Bridgman, David Clarke. Stanford, California: Hoover
Institution, Stanford University, 1965. 120p. (Hoover Institution
Bibliographical Series, 19).

This compilation is based on the extensive German collection at the Hoover
Institution. Among the 907 references are some French, English and other items,
but the majority of references are to German language materials. *Une
bibliographie du Cameroun: les écrits en langue Allemande* (q.v.), is more
thorough, but contains only German-language materials and is less accessible.

481 Women and economic development in Cameroon.
Judy C. Bryson. Yaoundé: US Aid, 1979. 155p. bibliog. map.

Bryson reviews published and documentary material to develop a ninety-four

148

page essay on the position of women in Cameroon society. Agriculture, motherhood and nutrition, education, and women in the modern sector are the major headings. An annotated bibliography of 191 items is quite valuable. This publication may be difficult to locate, but it is a useful contribution to the study of women in Cameroon.

482 **German foreign policy, 1890-1914, and colonial policy to 1914: a handbook and annotated bibliography.**
Andrew R. Carlson.   Metuchen, New Jersey: Scarecrow, 1970. 333p.
Cameroon, as one of several German African colonies, is included in this reference.

483 **Dissertations on Cameroon.**
E. Mucho Chiabi. *Current Bibliography on African Affairs*, vol. 14, no. 2 (1981-82), p. 88-97.
US, Canadian, African and European sources are included.

484 **La femme Camerounaise et le développement: bibliographie.** (The Cameroon woman and development: a bibliography.)
Michelle Dackey.   Addis Ababa: United Nations, Economic Commission for Africa, 1981. 70p. (Bibliography Series, no. 3).
The purpose of this volume of the special United Nations bibliographical series is to provide easy access to books, reviews, and publications for researchers interested in the role of women in development in Cameroon. Books are arranged alphabetically within six topical categories: general studies; population studies; health; legal and social conditions; education and professional status; and economics.

485 **A bibliography of Cameroon.**
Mark W. DeLancey, Virginia H. DeLancey.   New York: Africana, 1975. 673p. bibliog.
An annotated, multidisciplinary bibliography which includes more than 6,000 monographs, essays within books, and journal articles. The time period covered is from the onset of German colonization (1884) to 1973. The references include German, French and English titles. Entries are arranged alphabetically within subject divisions. The book includes an ethnic, linguistic and geographic index, an author and personal name index, and a subject index.

486 **African international relations: an annotated bibliography.**
Mark W. DeLancey.   Boulder, Colorado: Westview Press, 1981. 365p. bibliog.
This is a general bibliography of African international relations. 2,840 works are arranged alphabetically by author within eleven general categories: 'African international relations: general works;' 'African states foreign policies;' 'Inter-African conflicts, borders, and refugees;' 'Sub-continental regionalism;' 'The

Bibliographies

OAU, Pan-Africanism, and African unity;' 'The UN and international law;' 'Southern Africa;' 'The USSR, the PRC, the UK, and France: relations with Africa;' 'The USA: relations with Africa;' 'Other states: relations with Africa;' and 'Economic factors in African international relations.' Works are indexed according to subject.

487 A bibliography of Cameroun folklore.
Virginia H. DeLancey, Mark W. DeLancey. Waltham, Massachusetts: African Studies Association, 1972. 69p. bibliog.

Gathered for specialists of Cameroon folklore, the 500 entries were gleaned from national libraries and archives in the United States, England, and Cameroon. The entries are arranged alphabetically by author and include short summaries. The entries are indexed by specific genre of folklore and by ethnic identification.

488 Une bibliographie du Cameroun: les écrits en langue Allemande. (A bibliography of Cameroon: works in German.)
Max F. Dippold, preface by M.-S. Eno Belinga. Yaoundé: Editions CLE, 1971. 343p. bibliog.

This bibliography includes over 6,000 references of material written in the German language. The author was a German Lycee instructor in Nkongsamba from 1962 to 1967, and he then taught at the Ecole Normale Supérieure de Yaoundé. Brief sections include 'Works and brochures,' 'Doctoral theses,' 'Memoires,' and 'General works.' The major portion of the references are divided by subheadings under a section entitled 'Periodical articles.' A subject index facilitates access to listings. Also included is a small appendix which lists the major depositions (23) and works listed in the book which can be found there. This appendix is not comprehensive, however, pertaining only to the works the author readily had at hand.

489 A select bibliography of music in Africa.
L. J. P. Gaskin. London: International African Institute, 1963. 83p. (African Bibliography Series B).

This bibliography, although dated, provides a useful summary of music in Africa, with several references pertaining to Cameroon.

490 A bibliography of African art.
L. J. P. Gaskin. London: International African Institute, 1965. 120p. (Africa Bibliography Series B).

Author, subject, and geographical/ethnic indexes make this reference work easy to use.

150

491 **International African bibliography: current books, articles and papers in African studies.**
Edited by David Hall.   London: Mansell, for the Library of the School of Oriental and African Studies and the International African Institute, 1973- . quarterly.
This very useful compilation was originally published as part of *Africa, Journal of the International African Institute* (1929-1972) and then independently. It now reappears as part of the journal. It is especially useful for the humanities and social sciences.

492 **Bibliographie choisie d'écrits en sciences sociales et humaines sur le Cameroun.** (Selected bibliography of works in the social and human sciences on Cameroon.)
Hans F. Illy. In: *Kamerun*. Edited by Hans F. Illy.   Mainz, GFR: Hase and Koehler Verlag, 1974, p. 317-43.
This bibliographic list includes items in German, English, and French. Major subject headings are demography, geography, history, politics, economy, law, education, linguistics, religion, rural development, sociology/anthropology, urban areas, and geographic regions.

493 **Nigeria and Cameroon: an annotated bibliography.**
Modupe Irele.   Lagos: Libriservice, 1984. 67p. bibliog.
Conflict over borders is a frequent problem for Cameroon and Nigeria, and in 1981 this almost caused war. This source notes items, including newspaper references, on the incident, although the publication presents only the Nigerian point of view.

494 **Introduction to the study of Cameroon: a bibliographic essay.**
Victor T. LeVine. In: *Historical dictionary of Cameroon*. Victor T. LeVine, Roger P. Nye.   Metuchen, New Jersey: Scarecrow Press, 1974, p. 139-98.
A brief essay is followed by an extensive list of references to books and published essays.

495 **African trade unionism: a bibliography with a guide to trade union organizations and publications.**
George R. Martens.   Boston, Massachusetts: G. K. Hall, 1977. 119p. bibliog.
Provides much needed information on the subject, and contains several references to Cameroon.

Bibliographies

496 **Liste des thèses sur le droit Africain soutenues ou en préparation dans les universités Françaises depuis 1974.** (List of theses on African law completed or in preparation in French universities since 1974.)
P. F. Ngayap. *Droit Africain*, 2, (1982), p. 34-35. bibliog.
This bibliography, which includes references to Cameroon, is useful to the scholar interested in African law as viewed from the French perspective.

497 **Quelques sources bibliographiques du Cameroun.** (Some bibliographical sources of Cameroon.)
Martin Njikam. In: *The bibliography of Africa*. Edited by J. D. Pearson, Ruth Jones. New York: Africana; London: Cass, 1970, p. 113-19. bibliog.
Lists previous bibliographies either completely or significantly about Cameroon as well as mentioning several forthcoming works.

498 **Bibliographies for African studies 1980-1983.**
Yvette Scheven. New York, London, Paris: Hans Zell, 1984. 300p. bibliog.
This general reference to recent bibliographies of Africa contains 1,192 annotated entries. Items with a specific Cameroon section are listed in the index. Earlier bibliographies are included in two previous editions for 1970-1975 and for 1976-1979 published by Crossroads Press in 1977 and 1980.

499 **Periodicals from Africa: a bibliography and union list of periodicals published in Africa.**
Carole Travis, Miriam Alman. Boston, Massachusetts: G. K. Hall, 1977. 619p. bibliog.
Arranged by country. It is exceedingly difficult to keep up-to-date with the rapidly changing periodicals' situation in Cameroon. This reference, arranged by country, is helpful, though out of date.

500 **A bibliography of Cameroon.**
Diego Ungaro. In: *The political economy of Cameroon*. Edited by Michael G. Schatzberg, I. William Zartman. Baltimore, Maryland: Johns Hopkins University Press, 1986, p. 218-38.
This list of references on political and economic topics covers journal articles books and documents published up to and including 1984.

501 **Bibliography of the Summer Institute of Linguistics, 1935-1975.**
Alan C. Wares. Dallas, Texas: Academic Publications, Summer Institute of Linguistics, 1979. 317p. bibliog.
The Summer Institute of Linguistics (SIL) transcribes African languages so that the Bible and other Christian works can be read by a large African population

152

SIL has been active in Cameroon for many years. An update of this bibliography has recently become available. See Société Internationale de Linguistique, *Bibliographie des ouvrages de la SIL au Cameroun jusqu'en 1985* (Yaoundé: 1985. 44p).

502 **The United States and Africa: guide to US official documents and government sponsored publications on Africa, 1785-1975.**
Julian W. Witherell.   Washington, DC: Library of Congress, 1978. 949p. bibliog.
Country listings, divided into subjects for later years, are provided. A wide variety of subjects are included.

Language and society in West Africa.
See item no. 147.

La situation linguistique au Cameroun. 1. coup d'oeil sur les langues 2. aspects sociolinguistiques. (The Cameroon linguistic situation. I. a glance at the languages 2. sociolinguistic aspects.)
See item no. 158.

Index

The index is a single alphabetical sequence of authors (personal and corporate), titles of publications and subjects. Index entries refer both to the main items and to other works mentioned in the notes to each item. Title entries are in italics. Numeration refers to the items as numbered.

157

Bassa
    oral traditions 433
Le bassin camerounais de la Bénoué et
    sa pêche 377
Bassoro, Ahmadou 85
Bata 66, 91
Bati 20
Baxter, P. 43
Bayart, J-F. 233-235, 266, 464
Beauvilain, A. 207
Bebey, F. 409, 420-421
    novels 420-421
Because of women 430
Bederman, S. H. 352-353, 363, 370
Beer, G. L. 86
Bejeng, Pius Soh 40
Bekombo, Manga 203
Belgium
    military operations during World
        War I 123
Beling-Nkoumba, D. 129
Belinga, E. 236
Belinga, M.-S. E. 488
Bell, Douala Manga 117
    biography 117
    execution 81
Belloncle, G. 364
'The beloved' an Iowa boy in the
    jungles of Africa 171
Bender, C. 422
Benedictine Museum of Mont-Febe
    411
Benefit-cost analysis of measles
    vaccinations in Yaoundé,
    Cameroon 200
Benjamin, J. 237-238
Benjamin, N. C. 356
Bennett, J. 409
Benue (Bénoué) 16
Benue (Bénoué) River 19
    fishing industry 377
Benue (Bénoué) wildlife reserve 31
Beti 38
    agriculture 105
    initiation rite 136
    interviews with Beti women 76
    magic and sorcery 76
    oral traditions 433
    pre-colonial history 76
    role of women in food production
        105
    society 136

warfare 136
    women – attitude to Christianity 76
    women – groundnuts farming 371
Béti, Mongo 238, 266, 423-427
    novels 419, 423-427, 429, 433, 443
Beull, R. L. 87
Bibliographie choisie d'écrits en
    sciences sociales et humaines sur le
    Cameroun 492
Bibliographie des ouvrages de la SIL
    au Cameroun jusqu'en 1985 501
Une bibliographie du Cameroun: les
    écrits en langue Allemande 480,
    488
Bibliographies 8, 479-502
    agriculture 481, 485, 488
    anthropology 485, 488, 492
    art 490
    bibliographies 497-498
    border conflict with Nigeria 493
    boundaries 486, 493
    censuses 476
    demography 492
    economic development 335, 479
    economy 492, 500
    education 492
    folk tales 440, 487
    geography 492
    German colonialism 480, 482
    history 116, 128, 492
    international relations 486
    languages 147
    law 492, 496
    libraries – West Africa 474
    linguistics 158, 492, 501
    literature 429
    music 489
    Pahouin 38
    peoples of Southern Cameroon 49
    periodicals 499
    politics 500
    publishing and printing 470, 472
    religion 492
    rural development 492
    social sciences 492
    sociolinguistics 158
    sociology 492
    statistics 476
    theses and dissertations 483, 488,
        496
    towns 492
    trade unions 495

160

U.S. official documents 502
West Cameroon 479
women 481, 484
writers 453
Bibliographies for African studies 1980-1983 498
Bibliography of Africa 497
Bibliography of African art 490
Bibliography of Cameroon 485, 500
Bibliography of Cameroun folklore 487
Bibliography of the Summer Institute of Linguistics, 1935-1975 501
Bibliography of West Cameroon: economic development literature 479
Bidzar 122
Bikia, A. 455
Bikoi, C. B. 428
Bilabi (dance) 136
Bilingualism 156, 395, 404
Billard, P. 9
Bimbia 177
Binet, J. 38, 188
Biographies
  Ahidjo, Ahmadou 248
  Atangana, Charles 137
  Bell, Douala Manga 117
  Biya, Paul 227, 247
  Evans, R. H. 173
  Fon of Bafut 71
  Kale, P. M. 111
  Lewis, Mrs. T. 169
  Lewis, T. 177
  McCleary, C. W. 171
  Saker, A. 183
  Samba, Martin 84
  Sudan Mission Missionaries 168
  Sultan Njoya 132, 137
Biou 122
Birds 24, 28, 30
  Africa, West 24, 28
  West African town and garden species 28
Birds of French Cameroon 30
Birds of the West African town and garden 28
Bismarck Fountain, Buea 79
Biya, Paul 239, 247, 254, 274, 278, 287, 289, 328
  biographies 227, 247
  political philosophy 227, 247, 287

programme of national integration 247
reorganization of Cameroon National Union (CNU) 289
speeches 227
Biyiti bi Essam, J-P. 239
Black Africa develops 333
Black sheep, adventures in West Africa 178
Blasons Peuls: éloges et satires du Nord-Cameroun 447
Boateng, E. A. 310
Bockel, A. 240
Bodiman 49
Bona Ngombe
  subsistence activities 370
Book trade of the world. Vol. IV: Africa 468
Bookselling *see* Publishing and Printing
Boorman, J. 25
Booth, A. H. 26
Bornu empire 286
Bot ba Njock, H. M. 146
Bota *see* Victoria/Bota
Boundaries 311, 313, 319
  agreement between Germany and Great Britain (1893) 102
  bibliographies 486, 493
  Cameroon–Central African Republic boundary 319
  encyclopaedia 311
  history 313
  with Congo (Brazzaville) 319
  with Gabon 319
  with Nigeria 319
Bournard, L. A. 153
Bourou 66
Boutrais, J. 45, 88, 207
Bowls 418
Boy! 448
Brain, R. 41-42, 97, 410
Brann, D. M. B. 147
Brench, A. C. 429
Breton, R. 148-149
Briat, R. 103
Bridgman, J. 480
Brief history of the Bakweri 111
Britain
  capture of Yaoundé from Germans 123
  colonial education policy 394, 397

cooperatives 386
exports 138
Union of Cameroon Arabica Coffee
Cooperatives (UCCAO) 386
Coffee farming
Bakosi (Bakossi) 67
Cohen, W. B. 93
Colonial policy
Germany 108
Colonialism 83, 86-87, 110, 128-129,
139, 144, 286
administration 88
archives 477
bibliographies 480, 482
British 80, 87, 91-92, 96, 112, 119,
135, 252, 262, 286, 290, 397
encyclopaedias 103
French 18, 87, 93, 96, 100-101,
103-104, 106-107, 109, 135,
250-251, 253, 256, 262-263, 271,
332, 385, 451
German 80-81, 83-84, 86, 90, 92,
95-96, 98-99, 101-102, 107-108,
114, 117-119, 124, 132, 138,
140-141, 251-252, 263, 286, 316,
343, 432
German literature 432
'middlemen' 82-83
resistance to German rule 117
role of missionaries 110
taxation 106
training of French administrators 93
La colonisation des plaines par les
montagnards au nord du
Cameroun (monts Mandara) 88
Colonization 20, 88
Comarmond, P. de 388
Commerce 208, 271, 327
Commercial development
French 250
Communes
Bamileke region 303
Communications 330, 346, 349, 469
Cameroons Development
Corporation (CDC) 352
statistics 458, 462
Community organization
Banyang 73
Complexes agro-industriels au
Cameroun 351
Congo (Brazzaville) 319
Conseil de l'Enseignment Supérieur et

de la Recherche Scientifique et
Technique 389
Conseil de l'Enseignement Supérieur et
de la Recherche scientifique et
Technique 389
Constitution 301
20 May 1972 276
(modified) 1979 276
documents 302
Federation 301-302
history 301
of East Cameroon within the
Federal Republic (1 November 1961)
of the Federal Republic of
Cameroon (1 September 1961) 302
of West Cameroon within the
Federal Republic (26 October
1961) 302
Les contes du Cameroun 428
Contribution à l'étude de la préhistoire
au Cameroun septentrional 121
Contribution de la recherche
ethnologique à l'histoire des
civilisations du Cameroun 56, 62,
77, 121, 126
Contribution to national construction
224
Cookery books 455-456
Cooksey, B. 393
Cooperatives 335, 363, 379, 384, 386
Bakweri Co-operative Union of
Farmers, Ltd. (BCUF) 363
banana 363, 379
coffee 386
credit 380-383, 387-388
history 384
Maka village 264
role of U.S. Peace Corps 383
traditional 381-383, 387-388
Union of Cameroon Arabica Coffee
Cooperatives (UCCAO) 386
Coopératives de Crédit Mutuel 387
Core culture of Nso 70
Costedoat, R. 253
Cotton 365, 375
Council for Mutual Economic
Assistance (CMEA) 459
Courade, C. 394
Courade, G. 11, 211-212, 351, 394
Crafts 412-414, 418
photographs 412
West Cameroon 190

significance of 'jihad' 78
social mobility 43
Tignere 126
women 51
Yola 131
Fulani hegemony in Yola (old
Adamawa), 1809-1902 131
Fulbe Hooseere: les royaumes Foulbe
du plateau de l'Adamaoua au XIX
siècle: Tibati, Tignère, Banyo,
Ngaoundéré 126
Fulfulde language 125-127
folk tales 440
Fulfulde tales of Northern Cameroon II
440
Funeral urns
role in Mukulehe life 65
Fungom chiefdom 46
Futures Group, Resources for the
Awareness of Population Impacts
on Development (RAPID) 198

G

Gabelmann, E. 384
Gabon 319
Gailey, H. 477
Game preserves *see* wildlife reserves
Gann, L. H. 99
Gardinier, D. E. 100, 477
Garine, I. de 54
Garoua
Fulani (Fulbe, Foulbe) 126
history 85
Gaskin, L. J. P. 489-490
Gaullist Africa: Cameroon under
Ahmadou Ahidjo 266
Gauthier, J. G. 55
La Gazette 465
Gbaya 44, 57, 89
family life 57
Karnu rebellion 89
language 57
life and customs 57
literature 57
magic 57
mythology 57
myths and legends 57
nationalism 89
religion 57
social change 44

social structure 44, 57
Les Gbaya 57
Gebauer, Clara
private art collection 416
Gebauer, Paul 56, 408
private art collection 416
Gemjek
folklore 441
oral traditions 441
Genealogical tables
Bantu 39
Fulani (Fulbe, Foulbe) 125, 127
General report. The economic potential
of West Cameroon, priorities for
development. Vol. 1. 346
Die Genossenschaften in Kamerun: ihre
Entwicklung und ihre Bedeutung
für die wirtschaftliche und soziale
Entwicklung des Landes 384
Genuine intellectual 396
Geographical Distribution of Financial
Flows to Developing Countries
459
Géographie du Cameroun 10
Geography 3-5, 7, 9-14, 22
Bamenda 46
bibliography 492
economic 9
human 9-10, 14
maps and atlases 10, 11, 14
Ngemba chiefdoms 40
North Western Cameroon 38
physical 9-10, 14
political 310
rural 209
social 14
textbooks 10, 14
urban development of Buea 211
urban development of Victoria/Bota
212
West Cameroon 190, 209
Western province 11
Geology 13
German Africa: a select annotated
bibliography 480
German foreign policy, 1890-1914, and
colonial policy to 1914: a
handbook and annotated
bibliography 482
Germans in the Cameroons,
1884-1914: a case study in modern
imperialism 138

173

Germany
  19th century colonization 20
  annexation of Cameroon
      (1883-1887) 80, 141
  annexation of colonies by allies in
      World War I 119
  bibliographies – colonialism 480, 482
  colonial education 90
  colonial literature 432
  colonial policy 108, 141
  colonialism 80-81, 83-84, 90, 92,
      95-96, 99, 107-108, 114, 117, 124,
      138, 141, 252, 286
  colonialism – archives 478
  conflict with the Duala (1900-14) 81
  demands for return of African
      colonies in interwar period 118
  division of African colonies after
      World War I 118
  economic interests 108
  economic organization 96
  missionaries 180
  social structure of colonial
      administrators 99
  relations with Britain (1884-1914)
      119
  use of forced labour in plantations
      95
Geschiere, P. 263-264
Ghana 294
Gledhill, D. 29
Gonidec, P. F. 302
Good, A. I. 30
Good foot 438
Goray 122
Gouellain, R. 101
Government 301
  Banyang 73
  Kom 279
  Nso 70
  one-party system 261
  policies 286
  recruitment 278
  relations with foreign businessmen
      and investors 277
  relations with local government
      275
  repression 259
  rural development programmes 264
  Southern Cameroons House of
      Chiefs 92, 280
  West Cameroon 230

Government policy
  reports of Cameroon National
      Union Congress 242-243, 246
Graffenried, C. de 441
Grammar
  Duala 153
  Pidgin English 151, 159
Grammaire du Duala 153
Grammar of the Adamawa dialect of
      the Fulani language 164
Le grand livre de la cuisine
      Camerounaise 455
'Grands corps' 278
Grasslands see Western Grassfields
Gray, L. H. 86
Great Britain and Germany's lost
      colonies, 1914-1919 119
Great Britain. Historical Section,
      Foreign Office 102
Green, P. 424
Green, R. H. 266, 332
Green Revolution 367
Greenberg, J. H. 152
Greenough, R. 466
Grimaldi, J. 455
Groundnuts 371
Le group dit Pahouin (Fang-Boulou-
      Beti) 38
Growing out of poverty 197
Guernier, E. 103
Guidar 66
  culture 66
  economic life 66
  language 66
  social organization 66
Guidar, Northern Cameroon 74
Guide to Cameroon art from the
      collection of Paul and Clara
      Gebauer 416
Guillaume, G. M. D. 12, 370
Guinea 294
Guisiga 66
  culture 66
  economic life 66
  language 66
  social organization 66
Gunderson Mission see Sudan Mission
      of the Evangelical Lutheran
      Church
Gutkind, P. C. W. 318
Guyer, J. I. 104-106, 371, 385
Gwan, E. 217

174

H

Habitat
  influence on evolution by urban and rural planning 35
L'Habitation des Fali: montagnards du Cameroun septentrional 63
Haggblade, S. 382
Hall, D. 491
Hallaire, A. 372, 378
Halldén, E. 107
Halsey, A. W. 171
Hance, W. A. 333
Handbook of West African art 408
Happold, D. C. D. 31
Harper's Magazine 435
Hartwig, G. W. 95
Hausen, K. 108
Hawker, G. 169
Hazlewood, A. 230
Head tax, social structure, and rural incomes in Cameroun: 1922-1937 106
Health 202, 328, 332
  French Cameroon (1920s) 201
  Mount Cameroon forest areas 370
  plantation workers 205, 359
  statistics 460
Health and medicine. The economic potential of West Cameroon, priorities for development, Vol. 2. 202
Health services 296
  organization in French Cameroon 201
Hebga, M. P. 170
Hermet, G. 234
Hertslet, E. 313
High Court of Justice 276
Higher education 389
  Cameroon College of Arts, Science and Technology (CCAST) 400
  Conseil de L'Enseignement Supérieur et de la Recherche Scientifique et Technique 389
  role of universities in developing countries 396
Hilberth, J. 57
Hinkhouse, J. F. 171
Histoire de Garoua: cité Peule du XIX siècle 85
Histoire de l'église en Afrique

(Cameroun) 184
L'Histoire de Tibati: chefferie Foulbe du Cameroun 124
Histoire des forces religieuses au Cameroun: de la première guerre mondiale à l'independence (1916-1955)
L'Histoire des Peuls Ferobe du Diamare, Maroua et Pette 125
Histoire du Cameroun 128
Histoire et coutumes des Bamum 69
Historical dictionary of Cameroon 116, 494
Historical notes on the scheduled monuments of West Cameroon 79
History 3-5, 7, 14, 21-23, 78-144, 229, 255
  5th-11th century 122
  18th-20th century 82
  19th century 20, 78, 80, 85, 102, 114, 117, 126, 133, 136, 177
  19th-20th century 83-84, 95, 99, 107-108, 112, 114, 131-132, 138, 166, 174
  20th century 81, 86-87, 91, 102, 104, 106, 110-111, 117, 120, 130, 135, 142, 178, 180, 271-272, 280, 308
  Adamawa (Adamaoua) 112
  Africa 94
  Ahidjo régime 7, 224-226, 232, 249, 261, 266
  Ahidjo's attempted coup (6 and 7 April 1984) 239, 258
  Ahidjo's rise to power (1958-76) 235
  American Presbyterian Mission 186
  Anglo-French partition 251
  anti-colonialism 141
  Atangana, Charles 137
  attempted expropriation of Duala urban landholdings 81
  Bafut 71
  Bakosi (Bakossi) 52, 115
  Bamum (Bamoun) 69
  banana production 363, 379
  Baptist Church 175
  Basel Mission 107
  Bell, Douala Manga (execution) 81, 117
  Beti 105, 136
  Beti women 76
  bibliographies 116, 128, 492
  Biya régime (1982-) 287, 289

175

180

183

184

social organization 66
Mount Cameroon 12, 19
    ascent by A. Saker (1861-62) 183
    ecology 36
    flora 34
    forest vegetation 34, 36
    grassland vegetation 34
    health – forest areas 370
    nutrition – forest areas 370
    plantations 213
    subsistence activities in villages 370
Mountaineering 12
Mousgoum 66
    culture 66
    economic life 66
    language 66
    social organization 66
Moyen-Logone (Middle Logone) 45
    living conditions 45
Mukete, V. 181, 352
Mukulehe 65
    life and customs 65
    myths and legends 65
    Northern Cameroon 65
    role of 'funeral urns' 65
    social life 65
    supernatural beliefs 65
*Mukulehe: un clan montagnard du
    Nord-Cameroun* 65
Muna, S. T. 181
Munshi 19
Musée de l'Homme (Paris) 69
Museums 475
    Bamum 475
    Benedictine Museum of Mont-Febe
        411
    Diamaré 475
    Douala 475
    National Museum of Yaoundé 411
Music 2, 5, 328, 409
    Africa 409
    bibliographies 485, 488-489
    discography 409
    Fulani (Fulbe, Foulbe) women 51
    traditional 409
Musicians 409
    Bebey, Francis 409
Mveng, E. 52, 128-129, 414
Mwan' Ngoe Youth movement 52
Myths and legends
    Bamileke 37, 454
    Fali 63

Gbaya 57
Kirdi 63
Mukulehe 65

N

Nach Kamerun! 80
Namchi 66
Nanga, B. 446
    novels 446
*Nation and development in unity and
    justice* 225, 242
National Museum of Yaoundé 411
National security 8
*National union list of African
    development plans, censuses and
    statistical abstracts* 476
National unity 273
Nationalism 259, 273
    Bell, Douala Manga 117
    Cameroon Youth League 111
    Douala 101
    history 229, 285
    Karnu rebellion (Gbaya rebellion)
        89
    role of Duala 83
    Samba, Martin 84
    suppression by France (1950s) 259
    Union des Populations du Cameroun
        (UPC) 109
Nationality 301
Native problem in Africa 87
Natural gas 357
Natural resources 378
Ndeby, G. 394
Ndiki 50
    family life 50
    geographical location 50
    history 50
    life and customs 50
    society 50
Ndongko, W. A. 277, 315, 338-341
Ndongmo, Monseigneur Albert 238
Ndzong 40
Nelson, H. D. 8
Neo-colonialism 259-260, 285
    relations with France 260
New geography of Cameroon 14
New Noah 437
News agencies 469

189

194

195

196

197

199